√9५

CUMBER
&
WESTMORLAND

A GENEALOGICAL
BIBLIOGRAPHY

— BY —
STUART A. RAYMOND

FEDERATION OF FAMILY HISTORY SOCIETIES

10 661 8869

Published by the
Federation of Family History Societies,
c/o The Benson Room, Birmingham & Midland Institute,
Margaret Street, Birmingham, B3 3BS, U.K.

Copies also available from:
S.A. & M.J. Raymond, 6 Russet Avenue, Exeter, Devon, EX1 3QB, U.K.

Text processed and printed by
Oxuniprint, Oxford University Press

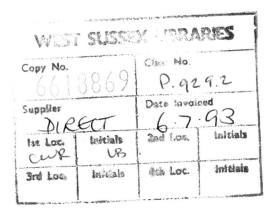

Cataloguing in publication data:

RAYMOND, Stuart A., 1945- .
Cumberland & Westmorland: a genealogical bibliography. British genealogical bibliographies.
Birmingham, England: Federation of Family History Societies, 1993.

DDC: 016.9291094278

ISBN: 1 872094 56 2

ISSN: 1033-2065

CONTENTS

INTRODUCTION

This bibliography is intended primarily for genealogists. It is hoped, however, that it will also prove useful to librarians, archivists, local historians, research students, and anyone else interested in the history of Cumberland and Westmorland families. It is designed to be used in conjunction with *English genealogy: an introductory bibliography*, which must be consulted on all the topics mentioned here at the national level, and with the other volumes in the *British genealogical bibliographies* series.

Many genealogists fail to appreciate just how much material likely to be of interest to them has been published. Not infrequently, they head straight for the archives, rather than checking the published literature first. When faced with the vast array of tomes found in record offices and libraries, they do not know where to begin. This bibliography is intended to point out the right direction. It is as complete as I have been able to make it.

My aim has been to list everything published on Cumberland and Westmorland that is likely to be of interest to the genealogist. In general, I have not included works which are national in scope, but which include Cumbrian material; such works may be identified in *English genealogy: an introductory bibliography*. I have also excluded the numerous notes and queries found in journals such as *C.F.H.S.N.*, except where the content is of some substance. Where I have included such notes, replies to them are given in the form 'see also', with no reference to the names of respondents. Local and church histories are excluded, except in a few cases. Such histories are frequently invaluable for genealogical purposes, but a full listing of them would require more space than is available. Newspaper articles are also omitted. This is a bibliography of published works only; hence the many unpublished works to be found in Cumbrian libraries are not listed here.

Be warned: I cannot claim that this bibliography is comprehensive. Neither do I claim total accuracy. Both are ideals to be aimed at, but no bibliographer can totally achieve them. I have physically examined most—but not all—of the works listed. Some works I have deliberately excluded; others I have undoubtedly missed. If you come across anything I have missed, please let me know, so that it can be included in a second edition in due course.

Be warned, too, that just because information has been published, it does not necessarily follow that it is accurate. I have not made any judgement on the accuracy of most works cited. That is up to you. If you are able, it is always best to check printed original sources against the original manuscripts, to see how well the editor did the job.

Most works listed here are readily available in the libraries listed below—although no library holds everything. Even if you are overseas, you should be able to find copies of the more important works in larger research libraries. However, if items prove difficult to locate, never fear! Librarians believe in the principle that all publications should be universally available, and most public libraries are able to tap into the international inter-library loans network. Your local library should be able to obtain most of the items listed here, even if it has to go overseas to get them.

The work of compiling this bibliography has depended heavily on the libraries I have used. These included the British Library, the Bodleian Library at Oxford, Exeter City Library, Exeter University Library, the Institute of Historical Research, Leeds City Library, the Brotherton Library, Leeds University, the Yorkshire Archaeological Society and the Cornwall Family History Society. I have also borrowed material by post from the Somerset and Dorset Family History Society. I am grateful to the librarians of all these institutions for their help. My thanks too to Joseph Hughes, who read and commented on an early draft of this book, and checked some citations for me, to Terry Humphries, who typed it, to Brian Christmas, who assisted with proof-reading, to Jeremy Gibson, for his support, and to Bob Boyd, who has seen it through the press.

Stuart A. Raymond

LIBRARIES AND RECORD OFFICES

The major collections of books and archives include:

Local Studies Library
Cumbria County Library
Arroyo Block
The Castle
CARLISLE
Cumbria CA3 8XF

Kendal Library
Strickland gate
KENDAL
Cumbria LA9 4PY

Cumbria Record Office
The Castle
CARLISLE
Cumbria CA3 8UR

Cumbria Record Office
County Offices
KENDAL
Cumbria LA9 4RQ

BIBLIOGRAPHIC PRESENTATION

Authors' names are in SMALL CAPITALS. Book and journal titles are in *italics*. Articles appearing in journals, and material such as parish register transcripts, forming only part of books, are in inverted commas and textface type. Volume numbers are in **bold** and the individual numbers, journal may be shown in parentheses. These are normally followed by the place of publication (except where this is London, which is omitted), the name of the publisher and the date of publication. In the case of articles, further figures indicate page numbers.

ABBREVIATIONS

C.F.H.S.	*Cumbria Family History Society*
C.F.H.S.N.	*Cumbria Family History Society Newsletter*
C.P.R.M.	*Cumberland Parish Registers: Marriages*
C.W.A.A.S.	*Cumberland and Westmorland Antiquarian and Archaeological Society*
C.W.A.A.S., E.S.	*Cumberland and Westmorland Antiquarian and Archaeological Society, Extra series*
C.W.A.A.S., P.R.S.	*Cumberland and Westmorland Antiquarian and Archaeological Society, Parish Register series*
C.W.A.A.S., R.S.	*Cumberland and Westmorland Antiquarian and Archaeological Society, Record series*
C.W.A.A.S., T.S.	*Cumberland and Westmorland Antiquarian and Archaeological Society, Tract series*
C.W.A.A.S., Tr.	*Cumberland and Westmorland Antiquarian and Archaeological Society, Transactions*
N.S.	New Series
P.P.R.S.	*Phillimore's Parish Register Series*

1. THE HISTORY OF CUMBERLAND AND WESTMORLAND

An appreciation of local history is essential if you want to know something about the way in which your ancestors lived, worked, ate, slept, and worshipped. If you want to understand the world of parish registers, probate courts and manorial records then you need to read up on local history. For Cumberland and Westmorland, a good place to begin is:

ROLLINSON, WILLIAM. *A history of Cumberland and Westmorland*. Darwen county history series. Chichester: Phillimore, 1978.

Two complementary works by C.M.L. Bouch should also be consulted:

BOUCH, C.M.L., & JONES, G.P. *A short economic and social history of the Lake counties 1500-1830*. Manchester: Manchester University Press, 1961.

BOUCH, C.M.L. *Prelates and people of the Lake counties: a history of the Diocese of Carlisle 1133-1933*. Kendal: Titus Wilson & Son, 1948. Includes a useful listing of mss. sources.

Only the first two volumes of the authoritative *Victoria county history* for Cumberland have so far been published:

WILSON, JAMES, ed. *The Victoria history of the County of Cumberland*. 2 vols to date. Archibald Constable & Co., 1901-5. Vol.1 includes the text of Domesday book (very brief), early pipe rolls, and the Testa de Nevill, etc. Vol.2 includes ecclesiastical history, monumental effigies, political history, industries, sport, and forestry.

Other general works include:

COLLINGWOOD, W.G. *The Lake counties*. Rev. ed. J.M. Dent & Sons, 1949. Originally published 1932. Includes extensive gazetteer omitted from original revised edition.

FERGUSON, RICHARD S. *A history of Cumberland*. Elliot Stock, 1890.

FERGUSON, RICHARD S. *A history of Westmorland*. Elliot Stock, 1894.

MILLWARD, ROY, & ROBINSON, ADRIAN. *The Lake District*. Eyre & Spottiswoode, 1970. Landscape history.

MARSHALL, J.D., & DAVIES-SHIEL, M. *The industrial archaeology of the Lake counties*. Newton Abbot: David & Charles, 1969.

ROYAL COMMISSION ON HISTORICAL MONUMENTS. *An inventory of the historical monuments in Westmorland*. H.M.S.O., 1936. Includes a brief armorial, notes on church monuments, etc.

Pre-twentieth century histories often provide much more information of genealogical relevance than more recent works. They frequently include monumental inscriptions, wills, extracts from parish registers, etc. One of the earliest Cumbrian historians was Sir Daniel Fleming, whose *Descriptions* of both counties provide brief ward surveys, and note the principal houses:

FLEMING, SIR DANIEL. *Description of the county of Cumberland*. ed. R.S. Ferguson. *C.W.A.A.S., T.S.* 3, 1889.

FLEMING, SIR DANIEL. *Description of the county of Westmorland ... A.D. 1671*. ed. Sir G.F. Duckett. *C.W.A.A.S., T.S.* 1, 1882.

Fleming's *Descriptions* are also printed in:

HUGHES, EDWARD, ed. *Fleming-Senhouse papers*. Cumberland record series 2. Carlisle: Cumberland County Council, [1962]. This also includes a rental of the Dean and Chapter of Carlisle, 1685/6, listing many Cumbrian tenants.

The collections of another 17th century antiquary were extensively used by later historians, and are printed in:

EWBANK, JANE M., ed. *Antiquary on horseback: the first publication of the collections of the Rev. Thos. Machell, chaplain to King Charles II, towards a history of the Barony of Kendal. C.W.A.A.S., E.S.* 19, 1963. Includes many monumental inscriptions, coats of arms and pedigrees.

In the 18th century, two major Cumbrian histories were produced; both included parochial surveys, giving much genealogical information:

NICOLSON, JOSEPH, & BURN, RICHARD. *The history and antiquities of the counties of Westmorland and Cumberland*. 2 vols. W. Strahan & T. Cadell, 1777. This is indexed in: HORNYOLD-STRICKLAND, HENRY, ed. *Index to Nicolson and Burn's History and antiquities of the counties of Westmorland and Cumberland ... C.W.A.A.S., E.S.* 17, 1934.

HUTCHINSON, WILLIAM. *The history of the county of Cumberland, and some places adjacent, from the earliest accounts to the present time, comprehending the local history of the county, its antiquities, the origin, genealogy and present state of the principal families, with biographical notes ...* 2 vols. Carlisle: F. Jollie, 1794. Reprinted East Ardsley: E.P. Publishing, 1974.

Nicolson & Burn's work is supplemented by:

CURWEN, JOHN F. *The later records relating to North Westmorland or the Barony of Appleby. C.W.A.A.S., R.S.* 8, 1932. Includes extracts from a wide variety of sources.

History of Cumberland and Westmorland
continued

Nineteenth and early twentieth century works with substantial genealogical information include:

DENTON, JOHN. *An account of the most considerable estates and families in the county of Cumberland, from the Conquest unto the beginning of the reign of K. James, [the first].* ed. R.S. Ferguson. *C.W.A.A.S., T.S.* **2**, 1887. Includes notes on many medieval families.

JACKSON, WILLIAM. *Papers and pedigrees mainly relating to Cumberland and Westmorland.* 2 vols. *C.W.A.A.S., E.S.* **5 & 6**, 1892. Reprints papers from various sources, including some pedigrees.

JEFFERSON, SAMUEL. *The history and antiquities of Cumberland, with biographical notices and memoirs.* 2 vols. Carlisle: S. Jefferson, 1840-42. Vol.1. Leath Ward. Vol.2. Allerdale Ward.

SANDFORD, E.S. *A cursory relation of all the antiquities and familys in Cumberland.* *C.W.A.A.S., T.S.* **4**, 1890. General survey of the county.

WHELLAN, WILLIAM. *The history and topography of the counties of Cumberland and Westmoreland, with Furness and Cartmel in Lancashire* ... Pontefract: W. Whellan & Co., 1860. A major parochial survey with lists of M.P.s, sheriffs, archdeacons, incumbents, etc., and many genealogical notes.

MOOR, C. 'The old statesman families of Irton, Cumberland', *C.W.A.A.S., Tr.* N.S. **10**, 1910, 148-98. Genealogical notes on many families.

Many scholarly books and articles on Cumbrian history have been written in recent years, and are worth reading—especially those based on genealogical sources. The following list is a personal selection; it is arranged in rough chronological order:

WINCHESTER, ANGUS J.L. *Landscape and society in medieval Cumbria.* Edinburgh: John Donald, 1987.

DENYER, SUSAN. *Traditional buildings and life in the Lake District.* Victor Gollancz, 1991.

HUGILL, ROBERT. *Castles and peles of Cumberland and Westmorland: a guide to the strongholds of the western English borderland* ... Newcastle on Tyne: F. Graham, 1977. Includes notes on occupants.

MCCARTHY, M.R., SUMMERSON, H.R.T., & ANNIS, R.G. *Carlisle Castle: a survey and documentary history.* English Heritage archaeological report **18**. Historic Buildings and Monuments Commission for England, 1990.

MARSHALL, J.D. 'Agrerian wealth and social structure in pre-industrial Cumbria', *Economic history review* 2nd series **33**, 1980, 503-21.

APPLEBY, ANDREW B. *Famine in Tudor and Stuart England.* Liverpool: Liverpool University Press, 1978. Largely based on Cumbrian parish registers. Important.

APPLEBY, A.B. 'Agrarian capitalism or seigneurial reaction? The North West of England 1500-1700', *American historical review* **80**, 1975, 581-94.

GREGSON, NICKY. 'Tawney revisited: custom and the emergence of capitalist class relations in north-east Cumbria 1600-1830', *Economic history review* 2nd series **42**, 1989, 18-42.

HOYLE, R.W. 'An ancient and laudable custom: the definition and development of tenant right in north-western England in the sixteenth century', *Past and present* **116**, 1987, 24-55.

TOUGH, D.L.W. *The last years of a frontier: a history of the Borders during the reign of Elizabeth.* O.U.P., 1928. Includes a list of wardens and a useful bibliographical introduction.

PHILLIPS, C.B. 'Town and country: economic change in Kendal c.1550-1700', in CLARK, P., ed. *The transformation of English provincial towns 1600-1800.* Hutchinson, 1984, 99-132.

SPENCE, R.T. 'The backward north modernised: the Cliffords, Earls of Cumberland, and the socage manor of Carlisle, 1611-1643', *Northern history* **20**, 1984, 64-87.

SPENCE, R.T. 'The pacification of the Cumberland borders, 1593-1628', *Northern history* **13**, 1977, 59-160.

MACFARLANE, ALAN. *The justice and the mare's ale: law and disorder in seventeenth-century England.* Oxford: Basil Blackwell, 1981. Important study of local government.

PHILLIPS, C.B. 'The Royalist North: the Cumberland and Westmorland gentry 1642-1660', *Northern history* **14**, 1978, 169-92.

PHILLIPS, C.B. 'The Royalist composition papers and the landed income of the gentry: a note of warning from Cumbria', *Northern history* **13**, 1977, 161-74.

MARSHALL, J.D. 'The rise and transformation of the Cumbrian market town, 1660-1900', *Northern history* **19**, 1983, 128-209.

BECKETT, J.V. *Coal and tobacco: the Lowthers and the economic development of West Cumberland 1660-1760.* Cambridge: Cambridge University Press, 1981. Includes brief pedigree, 16-18th c.

History of Cumberland and Westmorland
continued

MARSHALL, J.D. 'The domestic economy of the Lakeland yeoman, 1660-1749', *C.W.A.A.S., Tr.* N.S. **73**, 1973, 190-219. Based on probate inventories.

MARSHALL, J.D. 'Kendal in the late seventeenth and eighteenth centuries', *C.W.A.A.S., Tr.* N.S. **75**, 1975, 188-257.

COLLIER, SYLVIA. *Whitehaven 1660-1800: a new town of the late seventeenth century: a study of its buildings and urban development.* H.M.S.O., 1991. With a chapter on the role of the Lowther family.

DUXBURY, ARTHUR. 'Wealth and the standard of living in Ravenstonedale, 1691-1840', *C*, N.S. **85**, 1985, 219-27. See also **86**, 1986, 273-4. Based on probate inventories.

BECKETT, J.V. 'Absentee landownership in the late seventeenth and early eighteenth centuries: the case of Cumbria', *Northern history* **19**, 1983, 87-107. Includes map showing location of major estates.

HUGHES, EDWARD. *North country life in the 18th century, volume II: Cumberland and Westmorland 1700-1830.* Oxford University Press, 1965.

SEARLE, C.E. 'Custom, class conflict and agrarian capitalism: the Cumbrian economy in the eighteenth century', *Past & present* **110**, 1986, 106-133.

KINNEAR, MARY. 'The correction court in the Diocese of Carlisle, 1704-1756', *Church history* **59**, 1990, 191-206.

BONSALL, BRIAN. *Sir James Lowther and Cumberland and Westmorland elections 1754-1775.* Manchester: Manchester University Press, 1958.

MARSHALL, J.D., & DYHOUSE, CAROL A. 'Social transition in Kendal and Westmorland c.1760-1860', *Northern history* **12**, 1976, 127-56.

GRAHAM, T.B. *Nineteenth century self-help in education: mutual improvement societies. Vol.2. Case study: the Carlisle working men's reading rooms.* Nottingham: University of Nottingham Dept. of Adult Education, 1983. Includes a useful bibliography.

MARSHALL, J.D., & WALTON, JOHN K. *The Lake counties, from 1830 to the mid-twentieth century: a study in regional change.* Manchester: Manchester University Press, 1981.

THOMPSON, R.N. 'The working of the New Poor Law Amendment Act in Cumbria, 1836-1871', *Northern history* **15**, 1979, 117-37.

WILLIAMS, W.M. *The sociology of an English village: Gosforth.* Routledge & Kegan Paul, 1956. Cumberland.

2. BIBLIOGRAPHY AND ARCHIVES

This book is, of course, devoted primarily to genealogical publications relating to Cumberland and Westmorland. For a comprehensive bibliography on the general history of the two counties see:

HODGSON, HENRY WIGSTON. *A bibliography of the history and topography of Cumberland and Westmorland.* Carlisle: Joint Archives Committee for Cumberland, Westmorland and Carlisle, 1968. This excludes genealogical works, but includes many parochial histories not listed here.

For more recent journal articles, a comprehensive listing for the whole of Northern England is published annually. See:

'Review of periodical literature and occasional publications', *Northern history* 1-, 1966-.

Three more specialist bibliographies are:

POTTS, A., & JONES, E.R. *Northern labour history.* Library Association, Reference, Special and Information Section, 1981. Covers Durham, Northumberland and Cleveland as well as Cumbria; lists the archives of unions, friendly societies, political movements, etc., which include many lists of names.

ROWE, D.J., ed. *Northern business histories: a bibliography.* Library Association, Reference, Special & Information Section, 1979. Covers Cumberland, Westmorland, Co.Durham, Northumberland and Furness. Lists much mss. material as well as books and articles.

SPARKE, ARCHIBALD. *A bibliography of the dialect literature of Cumberland and Westmorland, and Lancashire north of the sands.* C.W.A.A.S., T.S. **9**, 1907. Lists many glossaries, dictionaries and local dialect works.

Theses submitted for higher degrees are usually ignored by genealogists, but sometimes contain much useful information. Those relating to Cumbria are listed in:

LAWLER, U.R.E. *North-West theses and dissertations, 1950-1978.* Lancaster: University of Lancaster Centre for North-West Regional Studies, 1979.

MCCLINTOCK, M.E., ed. *North-West theses and dissertations, 1979-84: a bibliography with subject and author indexes, 1950-1984.* [Lancaster]: [University of Lancaster], 1988.

Two important collections of books, manuscripts and prints, etc., relating to Cumbria are catalogued in:

HINDS, JAMES PITCAIRN. *Bibliotheca Jacksoniana: catalogue.* Kendal: Titus Wilson for Carlisle Public Library Committee, 1909.

CURWEN, JOHN F. *Topographical catalogue of the library at Horncop, Heversham, section 1: antiquities, archaeology, topography.* Kendal: Titus Wilson, 1907.

Archival sources should not be consulted until you have checked all relevant printed material. When you have done that, a useful introduction to Cumbrian archives for genealogists is:

GRISENTHWAITE, JIM. *Cumbrian ancestors: notes for genealogical searchers.* Kendal: Cumbria Archive Service, 1988.

A description of archival collections in the two counties—now rather out of date—is provided by:

JONES, B.C. 'Cumberland and Westmorland Record Offices, 1968', *Northern history* **3**, 1968, 162-71.

See also:

JONES, B.C. 'Local archives of Great Britain, XXVIII: Cumberland, Westmorland and Carlisle Record Office, 1960-1965', *Archives* 7(34), 1965, 80-86.

KIRKBY, J.L. 'A note on the Cumberland county records', *C.W.A.A.S., Tr.* N.S. **47**, 1947, 234-6. Brief description of records in what was the Cumberland County Record Office.

To update these descriptions, regular listings of accessions to Cumbrian repositories, amongst others, are provided in:

'Archive accessions', *Northern history* 1-, 1966-.

For notes on the manuscript collections of two antiquaries, see:

DUCKETT, SIR GEORGE. 'Westmorland: its tenures, general history, and post-mortem inquests exemplified in the collection of Rawlinson, among the mss. of the Bodleian Library', *C.W.A.A.S., Tr.* **4**, 1880, 13-14. Brief description of an important collection of mss.

MACHELL, RICHARD BEVERLEY. 'A notice of the late Mr. John Hill, of Bankfoot, and his Westmorland mss.', *C.W.A.A.S., Tr.* **9**, 1988, 14-28. Includes list of an antiquary's manuscript notes, with a folded pedigree of Hill, 16-19th c.

3. JOURNALS AND NEWSPAPERS

Every genealogist with ancestors from Cumberland or Westmorland should subscribe to:
Cumbria Family History Society newsletter 1976-.

This journal is essential, not just for reading, but also as the means by which you can make contact with others who may also be researching your ancestors. It includes extensive information on members interests.

An index is provided in:

RAMSDEN, NEVILLE. *Cumbria Family History Society: index for newsletters 1-40 (1976-1986).* [ ]: C.F.H.S., 1990.

The most important journal for Cumberland and Westmorland historians is:

Cumberland and Westmorland Antiquarian and Archaeological Society transactions. C.W.A.A.S., 1866-1900. N.S., 1901-.

This is indexed in:

CHERRY, JOYCE. *Index to the Transactions of the Cumberland and Westmorland Antiquarian and Archaeological Society, old series, vol.I to XVI (1866 to 1900).* Kendal: Titus Wilson & Son, 1981.

SPARKE, ARCHIBALD. *Catalogue-index to the transactions of the Cumberland and Westmorland Antiquarian and Archaeological Society: vol.I (1866) to vol.XVI (1900).* 1901.

SPENCE, C., & SPENCE, J.E. 'Author and subject index to the *Transactions* of the Cumberland and Westmorland Antiquarian and Archaeological Society, new series, volumes 1-45', *C.W.A.A.S., Tr.* N.S. **46**, 1946, 1-66. This is much less detailed than:

SCOTT, DANIEL. *An index-catalogue to the transactions (second series) of the Cumberland and Westmorland Antiquarian and Archaeological Society, vols.1 to 12 (1901 to 1912).* Kendal: Titus Wilson, 1915. i.e. new series.

COLLINGWOOD, W.G. *Index to the transactions of the Cumberland and Westmorland Antiquarian and Archaeological Society, new series, vol.XIII to XXV (1913 to 1925).* Kendal: Titus Wilson, 1928.

MELVILLE, J. 'Subject index to *Transactions* new series, volumes 46-72', *C.W.A.A.S., Tr.* N.S. **73**, 1973, 1-24.

CHERRY, JOYCE & CHERRY, JAMES. *Index to the Transactions of the Cumberland and Westmorland Antiquarian and Archaeological Society, new series, volumes 60 to 89 (1960 to 1989).* Stroud: Alan Sutton, [1991?].

The Cumberland and Westmorland Antiquarian and Archaeological Society is also responsible for publishing a number of series of record publications. Many individual volumes in these series are listed in subsequent sections below. They include:

Record series C.W.A.A.S., 1897-
Chartulary series (continued as *Tract series*) C.W.A.A.S., 1882-
Extra series C.W.A.A.S, 1877-

The publications of record societies are often of vital importance for the genealogist. The *Surtees Society*, which has as its remit the records of Northern England in general, has also published a number of volumes, listed individually in subsequent sections, which are of value to Cumbrian genealogists.

Many important articles on the general history of Cumbria appear in:

Northern history. Leeds: University of Leeds School of History, 1966-.

Useful notes on Cumbrian genealogy appeared in three short-lived journals of the late 19th/early 20th centuries:

Northern genealogist. 6 vols. York: John Sampson, 1895-1903.

Northern notes and queries: a quarterly magazine devoted to the antiquities of Northumberland, Cumberland, Westmorland and Durham. Newcastle upon Tyne: M.S. Dodds, 1906-7. One volume only issued.

The Westmorland note-book. 1 vol. Kendal: Edward Gill, 1888-9.

Local newspapers publish much useful information, especially in the births, marriages and deaths columns. Those for Cumbria are listed in:

BARNES, F., & HOBBS, J.L. *Handlist of newspapers published in Cumberland, Westmorland and North Lancashire.* C.W.A.A.S., T.S. **14**, 1951.

4. BIOGRAPHICAL DICTIONARIES, PEDIGREES, HERALDRY, ETC.

Amongst the most useful sources of genealogical information are the directories of members interests published by family history societies. These provide the names and addresses of their members, together with lists of surnames being researched. If yours is listed, you may be in luck! See:

CUMBRIA FAMILY HISTORY SOCIETY. *Directory of members interests*. C.F.H.S., 1987.

Biographical Dictionaries

Biographical dictionaries provide brief biographical information on the persons listed. Many are available, and are invaluable to the genealogist. For general guidance on identifying them, consult *English genealogy: an introductory bibliography*. Many are listed in *Occupational sources for genealogists*. Local works include:

ATKINSON, GEORGE. *The worthies of Westmorland, or, notable persons born in that county since the Reformation*. 2 vols. J. Robinson, 1849-50.

FULLER, THOMAS. *The history of the worthies of Cumberland and Westmorland*. Carlisle: S. Jefferson, 1839.

LONSDALE, HENRY. *The worthies of Cumberland*. 6 vols. George Routledge, 1867-75. Includes some relatively substantial biographies.

Visitation Pedigrees

In the sixteenth and seventeenth centuries, the heralds made 'visitations' of the counties to determine the rights of gentry to bear heraldic arms. One consequence of this activity was the compilation of pedigrees of most of the gentry. The heralds' returns continue to be important sources of genealogical information. They are edited in a number of works:

LONGSTAFFE, W. HYLTON DYER, ed. *Heraldic visitation of the northern counties in 1530, by Thomas Tonge, Norroy King of arms, with an appendix of other heraldic documents relating to the north of England*. Surtees Society, **41**, 1863. Covers Cumberland and Westmorland as well as Durham, Nottinghamshire and Yorkshire. See also: JABEZ-SMITH, A.R. 'A 17th-century version of Thomas Tonge's visitation of 1530', *C.W.A.A.S., Tr.* N.S. **78**, 1978, 85-96.

Visitation Pedigrees *continued*

FOSTER, JOSEPH, ed. *Pedigrees recorded at the heralds visitations of the counties of Cumberland and Westmorland made by Richard St.George, Norroy King of Arms in 1615, and by William Dugdale, Norroy King of Arms in 1666*. Carlisle: Chas. Thurnam & Sons, [1891?].

FETHERSTON, JOHN, ed. *The visitation of the county of Cumberland in the year 1615, taken by Richard St.George, Norroy King of arms*. Harleian Society publications **7**, 1872.

The heraldic visitation of Westmoreland made in the year 1615 by Sir Richard St.George, Knt., Norroy King of Arms. John Gray Bell, 1753.

See also:

FERGUSON, RICHARD S. 'Notes on the heraldic visitations of Cumberland and Westmorland', *C.W.A.A.S., Tr.* **2**, 1876, 20-27.

Heraldry

A number of works dealing with Cumbrian heraldry, including substantial armorials, are available. See:

FERGUSON, RICHARD S. 'The heraldry of Cumberland and Westmorland', *C.W.A.A.S., Tr.* **1**, 1874, 300-317.

FERGUSON, R.S. 'The heraldry of the Cumberland statesmen', *C.W.A.A.S., Tr.* **11**, 1893, 68-80.

FERGUSON, R.S. 'The heraldry of the Cumberland statesmen', *Archaeological journal* **48**, 1891, 77-82. Includes memorial inscriptions.

CURWEN, J.F. 'An index to the heraldry of Cumberland and Westmorland', *C.W.A.A.S., Tr.* N.S. **6**, 1906, 204-36. Includes index.

FIELD, F.J. *An armorial for Cumberland: a record of the arms, quarterings, crests, badges, supporters and mottoes borne by families resident or owning land within the county from the twelfth century to the present day, together with a history of local heraldry and some genealogical notes*. C.W.A.A.S., E.S. **18**, 1937.

BOUMPHREY, R.S., HUDLESTON, C. ROY, & HUGHES, J. *An armorial for Westmorland and Lonsdale*. C.W.A.A.S., E.S. **21**, 1975.

HUDLESTON, C. ROY, & BOUMPHREY, R.S. *Cumberland families and heraldry, with a supplement to An armorial for Westmorland and Lonsdale*. C.W.A.A.S., E.S. **23**, 1978. Includes genealogical notes on numerous families. See also: HUDLESTON, C. ROY, & BOUMPHBREY, R.S. 'A supplement to Cumberland families and heraldry', *C.W.A.A.S., Tr.* N.S. **81**, 1981, 27-47; **82**, 1982, 97-109; **83**, 1983, 73-84; **84**, 1984, 117-24.

Heraldry *continued*

An armorial of pre-1500 heraldry is printed in:
An inventory of the historical monuments in Westmorland. H.M.S.O., 1936.

BOUMPHREY, R.S. 'A Kirkby Lonsdale armorial', *C.W.A.A.S., Tr.* N.S. 7, 1971, 97-138.

See also:

ROBINSON, JOHN MARTIN. *A guide to the country houses of the North West*. Constable, 1991. By a Herald; includes much genealogical information.

5. OCCUPATIONAL SOURCES

Many works offer biographical information on persons of particular occupations. The list which follows may be supplemented by consulting my *Occupational sources for genealogists*. For clergymen, see below, section 12, for members of parliament and local government officers, section 14, for teachers and students, section 15.

Apprentices

RUSSELL, M.M. 'Greystoke apprentices', *C.F.H.S.N.* 37, 1984, 6-7. List, 1804-29.

SMITH, BARBARA H. 'Liverpool apprentices', *C.F.H.S.N.* 44, 1987, 15. Mainly from Kendal, early 18th c.

'Apprenticeship records', *C.F.H.S.N.* 35, 1985, 15; 36, 1985, 10. List of apprentices from stamp duty registers, 18th c. See also Sailors.

Brickmakers

JONES, B.C. 'Carlisle brickmakers and bricklayers, 1652-1752', *C.W.A.A.S., Tr.* N.S. 83, 1983, 125-9. Gives names.

Clockmakers

LOOMES, BRIAN. *Westmorland clocks and clockmakers*. Newton Abbot: David & Charles, 1974. Includes list with brief biographical details, plus much information, including pedigrees, on Barber and Philipson families.

HUGHES, T. CANN. 'Notes on some Westmorland clockmakers', *C.W.A.A.S., Tr.* N.S. 35, 1935, 42-55; 37, 1937, 147-51; 39, 1939, 171-89. Brief lists; pt.3 includes wills of the Barber family.

Cricketers

'A game of cricket in 1841', *C.R.H.S.N.* 8, 1978, 13-14. Names of Whitehaven and Maryport teams.

Freemasons

LAMONBY, WILLIAM FARQUHARSON. *History of craft masonry in Cumberland and Westmorland, from the year 1740 to the present day*. Carlisle: G. & T. Coward, 1879. Includes many names.

Millers

SOMERVELL, JOHN. *Water-power mills of South Westmorland on the Kent, Bela, and Gilpin and their tributaries*. Kendal: Titus Wilson & Son, 1930. Includes names of some millers.

Miners

CROSTHWAITE, J. FISHER. 'The colony of German miners at Keswick', *C.W.A.A.S., Tr.* **6**, 1883, 344-54. Gives some names.

HAMMERSLEY, GEORGE, ed. *Daniel Hechstetter the younger: memorabilia and letters, 1600-1639: copper works and life in Cumbria.* Stuttgart: Franz Steiner Verlag Wiesbaden GMBH, 1988. Includes much material on the mines and miners of the early 17th c., including many names.

WOOD, OLIVER. 'A colliery payroll in 1802', *C.W.A.A.S., Tr.* N.S. **72**, 1972, 303-18. Lists 453 miners, giving ages and some birthplaces.

Notaries

WILSON, JAMES. 'Some signatures of Carlisle notaries', *C.W.A.A.S., Tr.* **13**, 1895, 152-63. 16-17th c.

Pack Horse Men

JONES, B.C. 'Westmorland pack-horse men in Southampton', *C.W.A.A.S., Tr.* N.S. **59**, 1959, 65-84. Includes extracts from Southampton Cloth Hall accounts, 1552-3, giving names.

Pewterers

FINLAY, MICHAEL. 'The pewterers of Penrith', *C.W.A.A.S., Tr.* N.S. **85**, 1985, 163-86. Includes list of pewterers, with some biographical information.

Sailors

'Records of Brocklebank Shipping Line in Liverpool R.O. Ref.387, MD24: Whitehaven apprentices, 1808-1840', *C.F.H.S.N.* **25**, 1982, 10-11 & **26**, 1983, 20-21. List of apprentices giving ages.

'Twenty poor sailors', *C.F.H.S.N.* **44**, 1987, 8-10. List of beneficiaries, 1839-46, of charity created by the will of William Wilson, 1814.

Servants

BECKETT, JOHN. 'Some Cumbrian domestic servants, 1851-1881', *C.F.H.S.N.* **53**, 1989, 18. List giving ages, birthplaces, places of service, etc.

Shareholders

JARMAN, C. 'Merchant shipping', *C.F.H.S.N.* **24**, 1982, 9. Lists shareholders in Whitehaven ships, 1874 and 1876.

The deed of settlement (dated 2nd January 1837) of the Carlisle and Cumberland Bank ... to which is annexed a list of the shareholders. Carlisle: C. Thurnam, 1837.

'Small investors of yesterday', *C.F.H.S.N.* **44**, 1987, 11-12. Lists early 19th c. shareholders at Whitehaven.

Shepherds

'To every man his own', *C.F.H.S.N.* **34**, 1985, 3-8. Lists of shepherds, 1817 and 1848.

Soldiers and militiamen *etc.*

Many Cumbrians served in the army or the militia, and much information on them is available in the various regimental histories which have been compiled. These cannot all be listed here. The works noted below include only those publications which provide lists of officers and/or men, and which are therefore of direct genealogical interest. The list is in chronological order.

CANNON, RICHARD. *Historical record of the Thirty-Fourth, or, the Cumberland Regiment of Foot, containing an account of the formation of the Regiment in 1702, and of its subsequent services to 1844.* Parker, Furnivall & Parker, 1844. Includes notes on officers.

ARNISON, JANET. 'A roll of the Westmorland militia', *C.F.H.S.N.* **41**, 1986, 18. Brief roll, c.1779.

'Recruits for India', *C.F.H.S.N.* **48**, 1988, 16-17. List of troops recruited for the East India Company, 1779-86, from Cumberland and Westmorland; gives ages and occupation.

History of the 1st Cumberland Royal Garrison Artillery (Volunteers). Carlisle: Coward, 1902. Records of the various corps, with lists of officers, etc., 1860-1902.

HODGSON, J. 'The Cumberland Volunteer Artillery', *C.F.H.S.N.* **9**, 1978, 13-15. Nominal roll, 1868, of men from Whitehaven.

Soldiers died in the Great War, 1914-19. Part 39: the Border Regiment. H.M.S.O., 1921.

WYLY, H.C. *The Border Regiment in the Great War.* Aldershot: Gate & Polden, [1924]. Many names.

1st Battalion, the Border Regiment: nominal roll on embarkation for active service, March, 1915. Carlisle: Thurnam, 1915.

SHEARS, PHILIP J. *The story of the Border Regiment, 1939-1945.* Nisbet & Co., 1948. Includes full lists of officers, honours, etc.

Steelmakers

LANCASTER, J.Y., & WATTLEWORTH, D.R. *The iron and steel industry of West Cumberland: an historical survey.* Workington: British Steel Corporation, 1977. Includes useful list of sources.

Tradesmen

In an age when coins were in short supply, many tradesmen issued their own tokens. Studies of these often provide useful genealogical information. See:

BROCKETT, WILLIAM HENRY. *The tradesmen's tokens (of the 17th century) of Cumberland and Westmorland.* Gateshead: [ ], 1853.

Wrestlers

COWLEY, D.I. 'The Cumberland wrestling championship', *C.F.H.S.N.* **7**, 1978, 6-7. Many names, 1834-43.

'Carlisle wrestling 1839', *C.F.H.S.N.* **43**, 1987, 16-17. Many names of wrestlers, from an advertisement.

6. FAMILY HISTORIES, ETC.

Aglionby

GRAHAM, T.H.B. 'Annals of the Aglionbys', *C.W.A.A.S., Tr.* N.S. **33**, 1933, 24-33. 12-17th c., includes pedigree.

Akinson

See Atkinson

Allen

'Family register from the family bible of Miss O. Harding', *C.F.H.S.N.* **18**, 1981, 10-11. Allen family, 19-20th c.

Alsop

ALSOP, R.M. 'The Alsops', *C.F.H.S.N.* **49**, 1988, 7-9. 19th c.

Armitstead

COCKERILL, TIMOTHY. 'The Rev. Richard Armitstead of Whitehaven', *C.W.A.A.S., Tr.* N.S. **65**, 1965, 374-80. 18-19th c., includes notes on family.

Armstrong

ARMSTRONG, BERNARD. *Anglo-Scottish relations and the Border, B.C. to the 17th century, Celts to Stuarts.* Lymington: Clan Armstrong Trust, 1991. Armstrong family history.

Askew

HUDLESTON, C. ROY. 'Askew of Standing Stones', *C.W.A.A.S., Tr.* N.S. **79**, 1979, 57-74. Includes pedigrees, 16-17th c., wills and deeds.

MOOR, C. 'The Askews and Penningtons of Seaton', *C.W.A.A.S., Tr.* N.S. **11**, 1911, 167-84. 15-17th c., includes pedigrees.

See also Fell

Atkinson

ATKINSON, HAROLD WARING. *The families of Atkinson of Roxby (Lincs) and Thorne and Dearman of Braithwaite and families connected with them, especially Atkinson-Busfield, Barnes, Beavington, Birchall, Edwards, Miller, Neave, Ransome, Rooke, Sessions, Sinclair, Somerford, Stanley, Waring, Wykeham.* Northwood: the author, 1934. Includes various pedigrees, with extracts from Quaker minute books, etc.

HARPER, KENNETH. 'John Atkinson, 1773-1857: yeoman schoolmaster', *C.W.A.A.S., Tr.* N.S. **83**, 1983, 157-61. Includes pedigree, 18-19th c.

See also Huartston

Bainbrig

BROWN, R. PERCIVAL. 'Bainbrig of Hawkin in Middleton, Westmorland', *C.W.A.A.S., Tr.* N.S. **24**, 1924, 123-48. Includes folded pedigree, 16-18th c.

BROWN, R. PERCIVAL.. 'Thomas Langton and his tradition of learning', *C.W.A.A.S., Tr.* N.S. **26**, 1926, 150-246. Bainbrig family, 15-19th c., includes pedigrees and 36 documents, mainly wills.

Bankes

See Huartson

Barber

HUDLESTON, C. ROY. 'Jonas Barber, clockmaker and the Cookson and Elleray families', *C.W.A.A.S., Tr.* N.S. **71**, 1971, 286-7. Includes pedigrees, 18th c.

Barker

HAWORTH, CHRISTINE, & RICHARDSON, NORMAN. 'A chest in the dwelling house, and ark in the barn', *C.F.H.S.N.* **5**, 1989, 11-15. Barker family history; includes pedigree, 18-19th c.
See also Huartson

Barnes

See Atkinson

Barwis

FAHY, T.G. 'The Barwis family', *C.W.A.A.S., Tr.* N.S. **72**, 1972, 341-3. Includes brief pedigree, 18th c.

MACDONALD, ALEC. 'The family of Barwis', *C.W.A.A.S., Tr.* N.S. **37**, 1937, 106-29. Includes pedigrees (one folded), 13-20th c.

SWIFT, F.B. 'The Barwises of Lowsay', *C.W.A.A.S., Tr.* N.S. **46**, 1946, 157-73. Includes pedigree, 17-19th c., with wills.

SWIFT, F.B. 'Barwis of Cumberland', *C.W.A.A.S., Tr.* N.S. **50**, 1950, 135-51 & **51**, 1951, 117-36. Includes folded pedigrees, 14-17th c. and probate records.

Baynes

CHIPPINDALL, W.H. 'The Baynes family of Cockermouth', *C.W.A.A.S., Tr.* N.S. **35**, 1935, 30-6. 18th c., includes pedigree and wills.

CHIPPINDALL, W.H. 'Robert Baynes of Littledale in Caton, Co.Lancaster, standard bearer to Sir Edward Stanley at Flodden Field, and his descendants', *C.W.A.A.S., Tr.* N.S. **41**, 1941, 54-71. 15-19th c., includes pedigree.

Beavington

See Atkinson

Bewley

BEWLEY, SIR E.T. *The Bewleys of Cumberland and their Irish and other descendants, with full pedigrees of the family from 1332 to the present day.* Dublin: William McGee, 1902.

Binyon

COCKERILL, T.J. 'The Binyons', *C.F.H.S.N.* **42**, 1987, 15-16. 19-20th c.

Birchall

See Atkinson

Birkbeck

BIRKBECK, ROBERT. *The Birkbecks of Westmorland and their descendants.* Mitchell & Hughes, 1900. Medieval-19th c., includes pedigrees.
'Pedigree of Birkbeck of Hornby, Co.Westmorland', *C.W.A.A.S., Tr.* **5**, 1881, 346(f). Folded pedigree, 16-17th c.

Blencowe

CURWEN, J.F. 'Blencow Hall', *C.W.A.A.S., Tr.* N.S. **7**, 1907, 120-27. Includes folded pedigree of Blencowe, 14-19th c.

Blenkhouse

See Burden

Blenkinship

ROYLE, E.C. 'The Blenkinships', *C.F.H.S.N.* **25**, 1982, 7-9. 19th c. emigrant to Canada.

Blennerhasset

MORIARTY, G. ANDREWS. 'Genealogical research in England: the East Anglian Blennerhassets', *New England historical and genealogical register* 98(3), 1944, 271-9. Of Cumberland, Norfolk and Suffolk.
See also Kirkbride

Borradaile

B[ORRADAILE], A.F. *Sketch of the Borradailes of Cumberland.* Maclure & Macdonald, 1881. Includes pedigrees, 15-19th c., with extracts from parish registers.

Bouch

See Beuth

Boucher

BOUCH, C.M. LOWTHER. 'Jonathan Boucher', *C.W.A.A.S., Tr.* N.S. **27**, 1927, 117-51. Includes pedigree, 17-20th c.

Bowman

WHITEHEAD, H. 'Robert Bowman's supposed baptismal register', *C.W.A.A.S., Tr.* **5**, 1881, 33-8. 18-19th c.

Braddyll

CURWEN, JOHN F. 'Pedigree comprehending the descents of the families of Braddyll of Brockholes, Dodding of Dodding Green and Gale of Whitehaven ...', *C.W.A.A.S., Tr.* N.S. **8**, 1908, 382(f). Folded pedigree, 16-19th c. Brockholes, Lancashire; Dodding Green, Kendal.

Braithwait

WIPER, W. 'The arms in the window at High House, Hugill', *C.W.A.A.S., Tr.* **8**, 1886, 134(f). Folded pedigree of Braithwait, 16-17th c.

ROBERTSON, JEAN. 'Civil war in the Brathwait family', *C.W.A.A.S., Tr.* N.S. **38**, 1938, 138-45. 17th c. (nothing to do with the English Civil War).

Bromley

HUGHES, J. 'Bromleys of Keswick: a family business', *C.W.A.A.S., Tr.* N.S. **74**, 1974, 186-98. Includes pedigree, 18-20th c.

Brougham

ARNISON, MAJOR. 'The Brougham family', *Transactions of the Cumberland and Westmorland Association for the Advancement of Literature and Science* **17**, 1891-2, 85-9. 16-19th c.

DAVEY, C.R. 'Further sources for a study of the Brougham family', *C.W.A.A.S., Tr.* N.S. **67**, 1967, 112-24. Summary list of deeds relating to the Brougham and Richmond families, 17-18th c., includes wills and pedigree of Harrison, 16th c.

HUDLESTON, C. ROY. 'The Brougham family', *C.W.A.A.S., Tr.* N.S. **61**, 1961, 131-68. 17-18th c., includes folded pedigree, wills, etc.

Brown

VERITY, T.E.A., ET AL. 'The Browns of Burnfoot: the decline and fall of a yeoman family', *C.W.A.A.S., Tr.* N.S. **68**, 1968, 169-91. Includes pedigrees, 17-19th c., with probate records of Brown and Routledge, and list of deeds.

Browne

See Simpson

Brownrigg

CROSTHWAITE, J.F. 'Some old families in the parish of Crosthwaite: the Brownriggs of Ormathwaite', *Transactions of the Cumberland and Westmorland Association for the Advancement of Literature and Science* **13**, 1887-8, 31-46. 17-18th c.

Brunskill

BRUNSKILL, J. 'The Brunskills', *C.W.A.A.S., Tr.* N.S. **3**, 1903, 366-72. Brief note, 16-18th c.

Bueth

BOUCH, C.M. LOWTHER. 'A twelfth century Cumberland surname', *C.W.A.A.S., Tr.* N.S. **36**, 1936, 24-34. The Bueth or Bouch family; includes pedigree, 12-14th c.

Burden

'Early Cumberland and Westmorland pedigrees from the plea rolls', *Northern genealogist* **4**, 1902, 138-9 & **5**, 1903, 33-4. Includes pedigrees of Burden, Raughton, Stirkland, Blenkhouse, Southayk, Gervaes and Haltclough families; medieval.

Burdett

WATSON, GEORGE. 'The Burdetts of Bramcote and the Huttons of Penrith', *C.W.A.A.S., Tr.* N.S. **3**, 1903, 269-71. Bramcote, Warwickshire. Monumental inscriptions, with a pedigree, 17-19th c.

Burrough

BORROW, J.R.E. 'The Burroughs of Carleton Hall', *C.W.A.A.S., Tr.* N.S. **68**, 1968, 179-204. 18-19th c.

Burton

WATTS, M.J. 'The Burton family of clockmakers', *C.W.A.A.S., Tr.* N.S. **81**, 1981, 83-91. Includes pedigree, 17-19th c.

Busfield

See Atkinson

Carleton

CARLETON, LORNA. 'General Guy Carleton', *C.F.H.S.N.* **17**, 1980, 6-7. Includes pedigree, 16-18th c., showing descent of a governor of Quebec from a Cumberland family.

SCOTT, DANIEL. *The Carletons of Carleton Hall: sketch of the history of an old Cumberland family.* Penrith: R. Scott, 1898. Brief history, 14-18th c.

Carruthers

CARRUTHERS, A. STANLEY, & REID, R.C. *Records of the Carruthers family.* Elliot Stock, 1933. With supplement, 1958. Includes pedigrees, medieval-20th c.

Cartmar

JARMAN, CECIL. 'Cartmar family', *C.F.H.S.N.* **49**, 1988, 10-11. 17-19th c.

Carus

FAHY, T.G. 'The Carus family', *C.W.A.A.S., Tr.* N.S. **63**, 1963, 286-7. 18th c.

Chaloner

JACKSON, W. 'The Chaloners, lords of the manor of St.Bees', *Transactions of the Cumberland and Westmorland Association for the Advancement of Literature and Science* **6**, 1880-1, 47-74. 16-17th c.

Chambers

GRAINGER, FRANCIS. 'The Chambers family of Raby Cote', *C.W.A.A.S., Tr.* N.S. **1**, 1901, 194-234. Includes folded pedigrees, medieval-19th c., with extracts from parish registers, wills, etc., including the will of Thomas Fysher, 1548.

Christian

CURWEN, ALAN D. 'The Christians of Ewanrigg', *C.W.A.A.S., Tr.* N.S. **4**, 1904, 217-24. Includes folded pedigree, 15-19th c.

Clarel

See Fell

Clifford

DICKENS, A.G. *Clifford letters of the sixteenth century*. Surtees Society **172**, 1962.
The Clifford Association newsletter. Crawley: D.J.H. Clifford, 1983-
See also Vipont

Cookson

HEDLEY, W. PERCY, & HUDLESTON, CHRISTOPHE ROY. *Cookson of Penrith, Cumberland, and Newcastle upon Tyne*. Kendal: Titus Wilson & Son, 1968. Includes pedigree, 16-20th c.
See also Barber

Cooper

COOPER, G.M. 'The Coopers of Beckfoot, Ulpha', *C.W.A.A.S., Tr.* N.S. **64**, 1964, 349-55. Includes folded pedigrees, 17-19th c., and extracts from bishops' transcripts.

Correy

'[Pedigree of Correy]', *C.F.H.S.N.* **48**, 1988, 3. 18th c.

Cotton

See Fell

Coulthard

COULTHARD, JILL. '[Pedigree of Coulthard, 18-20th c.]', *C.F.H.S.N.* **56**, 1990, 11.

Cowen

See Trimble

Crackenthorpe

BOUCH, C.M.L. 'Newbiggin Hall, Westmorland', *C.W.A.A.S., Tr.* N.S. **54**, 1954, 140-43. Includes notes on the Crackenthorpe family, 15-16th c.

HUDLESTON, C. ROY. 'Crackenthorpe of Little Strickland: a footnote', *C.W.A.A.S., Tr.* N.S. **42**, 1942, 122-31. Includes pedigree, 18th c., and wills.

MOOR, C. 'Crackenthorp of Newbiggin', *C.W.A.A.S., Tr.* N.S. **33**, 1933, 43-97. 13-17th c., includes pedigrees (some folded).

SCOTT, DANIEL. 'Little Strickland Hall and its owners', *C.W.A.A.S., Tr.* N.S. **12**, 1912, 113-20. Includes notes on the Crackenthorpe family.

Crosfield

CROSFIELD, JOHN FOTHERGILL. *The Crosfield family: a history of the descendants of Thomas Crosfield of Kirkby Lonsdale who died in 1614.* [Cambridge]: [Cambridge University Press], 1980.

Cundal

RAGG, FREDERICK W. 'De Cundal, Bampton Cundal, and Butterwick', *C.W.A.A.S., Tr.* N.S. **22**, 1922, 281-328. Medieval; includes brief pedigrees, with deeds.

Curwen

CURWEN, JOHN F. *A history of the ancient house of Curwen, of Workington in Cumberland, being a collection of extracts from the monastic chartularies, inquisitions, wills, English and Scottish public records, Hist. mss. and other available sources.* Kendal: Titus Wilson & Son, 1928. Medieval-19th c.

JACKSON, W. 'The Curwens of Workington Hall and kindred families', *C.W.A.A.S., Tr.* N.S. **5**, 1881, 181-232 & 311-42. Includes folded pedigrees, 11-19th c., with deeds, probate records, parish register extracts, etc.

Dacre

PREVOST, W.A.J. 'Mary Lady Clerk's work-box', *C.W.A.A.S., Tr.* N.S. **73**, 1973, 220-25. Dacre family; includes pedigree, 17-19th c.
'The Dacre family', *C.W.A.A.S., Tr.* N.S. **11**, 1911, 258(f). Folded pedigree, 13-17th c.
See also Winder

Dalston

HASWELL, FRANCIS. 'The family of Dalston', *C.W.A.A.S., Tr.* N.S. **10**, 1910, 201-70. See also **49**, 1949, 222. Includes pedigrees, wills, etc.; 13-18th c.

HUDLESTON, C. ROY. 'The Dalstons of Acornbank', *C.W.A.A.S., Tr.* N.S. **58**, 140-79. Includes pedigrees, 17-18th c., deeds, wills, etc.

Deane
See Washington

Dearman
See Atkinson

De Beetham
CURWEN, J.F. 'Beetham Hall', *C.W.A.A.S., Tr.* N.S. **4**, 1904, 225-32. Includes pedigree of De Beetham, 13-15th c.

De Asmunderlaw
SKELTON, JOSEPH. 'The De Asmunderlaws of Furness and Cumberland', *C.W.A.A.S., Tr.* N.S. **39**, 1939, 59-64. Includes folded pedigree, 12-15th c.

De Boyvil
SYKES, W.S. 'The De Boyvils of Millum, and Kirksanton', *C.W.A.A.S., Tr.* N.S. **41**, 1941, 15-40. Medieval; includes pedigrees.

De Caupeland
SYKES, W.S. 'Ulf and his descendants', *C.W.A.A.S., Tr.* N.S. **41**, 1941, 123-51. De Caupeland family, medieval.

De Culwen
RAGG, FREDERICK W. 'De Culwen', *C.W.A.A.S., Tr.* N.S. **14**, 1914, 343-432. Includes folded medieval pedigree, with 28 deeds, etc.

De Multon
GRAHAM, T.H.B. 'The De Multons of Gilsland', *C.W.A.A.S., Tr.* N.S. **28**, 1928, 157-66. Medieval.

Denton
GRAHAM, T.H.B. 'The family of Denton', *C.W.A.A.S., Tr.* N.S. **16**, 1916, 40-56. Includes folded pedigree, 12-19th c.

GRAHAM, T.H.B. 'Analysis of the Denton pedigree', *C.W.A.A.S., Tr.* N.S. **33**, 1934, 1-16. Medieval-17th c., includes pedigrees.

Derwentwater
COLLINGWOOD, W.T. 'The home of the Derwentwater family', *C.W.A.A.S., Tr.* N.S. **4**, 1904, 257-87. Includes a rental of the manors of Castlerigg and Derwentwater, Cumberland, 1723.

THOMPSON, W.N. 'The Derwentwaters and Radcliffes', *C.W.A.A.S., Tr.* N.S. **4**, 1904, 288-322. Medieval-17th c.

Dickinson
BARNES, EUSTACE S. 'Dickinsons of Witherslack and Dawson Fold, Lyth', *C.F.H.S.N.* **57**, 1990, 18-22. Includes pedigree, 18th c.

Docker
LISSANT, GEORGE. 'A pedigree of the family of Docker of Keld (Shap), Bampton, Newby and Gosforth', *C.W.A.A.S., Tr.* N.S. **18**, 1918, 161-73. 16-17th c.

Dodding
See Braddyll

Dryden
MUNDY, P.D. 'The Cumberland ancestry of John Dryden', *Notes & queries* **180**, 1941, 290-1. 16-17th c.

Duckett
DUCKETT, SIR G.F. *Duchetiana, or, historical and genealogical memoirs of the family of Duket, from the Conquest to the present time, in the counties of Lincoln, Westmoreland, Wilts., Cambridge and Buckinghamshire* ... J. Russell Smith, 1874. Includes notices of Windesore family.

Dudley
JACKSON, W. 'The Dudleys of Yanwath', *C.W.A.A.S., Tr.* **9**, 1888, 318-32. Includes folded pedigree, 16th c.

Edwards
See Atkinson

Eglesfeld
MAGRATH, JOHN RICHARD. 'Fresh light on the family of Robert de Eglesfeld, founder of the Queen's College, Oxford', *C.W.A.A.S., Tr.* N.S. **16**, 1916, 239-79. Includes medieval pedigree.

Elleray
See Barber

Engayne
JACKSON, EDWIN. 'Clifton Hall and its owners', *C.W.A.A.S., Tr.* N.S. **12**, 1912, 135-42. Includes notes on Engayne and Wybergh families, medieval-19th c.

Farish
Family of Farish of Cumberland, formerly of Dumfriesshire. A.P. Blundell, Taylor & Co., 1902. 17-19th c.

Family of Farish of Holme Cultram in Cumberland. A.P. Blundell, Taylor & Co., 1898. 17-19th c.

Family Histories etc. continued

Fell

FELL, ALEXANDER LONSDALE. *Pedigrees of the family of Fell, of Knells in the county of Cumberland, connected with Lonsdale, Cotton, Hill, Noble, Gylby, Fitzwilliam, Clarel, Haig, Heywood, &c.* [ ]: [ ], 1907. 18-19th c.

Fetherstonhaugh

FETHERSTONHAUGH, MRS. 'The College of Kirkoswald and the family of Fetherstonhaugh', *C.W.A.A.S., Tr.* N.S. **14**, 1914, 196-237. 16-19th c., includes wills.

Fitzwilliam

See Fell

Fleming

MAGRATH, JOHN RICHARD. *The Flemings in Oxford, being documents selected from the Rydal papers in illustration of the lives and ways of Oxford men, 1650-1700.* 3 vols. Oxford Historical Society, **44**, **62** & **79**, 1904-24. Fleming family of Rydal, Westmorland.

BOUCH, C.M.L. 'Sir Daniel Fleming's courtship and marriage', *C.W.A.A.S., Tr.* N.S. **53**, 1953, 110-15. Includes pedigree, 17th c.

FLEMING, JOHN. 'Fleming of Newfield', *C.W.A.A.S., Tr.* N.S. **62**, 1962, 328-9. 17th c.

H[UDLESTON], C.R. 'Fleming of Newfield', *C.F.H.S.N.* **46**, 1988, 4-6 & **47**, 1988, 4-6. 16-18th c.

HUDLESTON, C.R. 'The Fleming family: the first and third baronets of Rydal', *C.W.A.A.S., Tr.* N.S. **64**, 1964, 264-305. Includes pedigree, 17-20th c., and wills, etc.

HUDLESTON, C. ROY. 'Fleming family memoranda from an old Bible', *C.W.A.A.S., Tr.* N.S. **56**, 1956, 142-3. 18th c.

Fletcher

'The Fletchers of Wasdale Head', *C.F.H.S.N.* **42**, 1987, 13-15. 17-18th c., includes pedigree.

Forster

FOSTER, JOSEPH. *A pedigree of the Forsters and Fosters of the north of England, and of some of the families connected with them.* 2nd ed. New Barnet: [ ], 1871. Includes pedigrees, 14-19th c.

HUDLESTON, C. ROY. 'The Forsters of Stonegarthside Hall', *C.W.A.A.S., Tr.* N.S. **61**, 1961, 169-201. Includes folded pedigree, 17-18th c., wills, schedule of deeds, extracts from bishops' transcripts, etc.

Foster

See Forster

Frear

CROSSFIELD, H.E. 'The Frear family of millers', *C.F.H.S.N.* **32**, 1984, 14. 19th c.

Fysher

See Chambers

Gale

SMITH, J.C.C. 'New notes on the ancestry of George Washington', *Genealogist* N.S. **7**, 1883, 1-3. Primarily concerned with Gale of Whitehaven; includes 18th c. pedigree of Gale.

See also Braddyll and Washington

Gervaes

See Burden

Gilpin

CROPPER, JAMES. 'Kentmere Hall', *C.W.A.A.S., Tr.* N.S. **1**, 1901, 280-84. Mainly concerns Gilpin family.

GILPIN, RICHARD. *Memoirs of Dr. Richard Gilpin, of Scaleby Castle in Cumberland, and of his posterity in the two succeeding generations, written, in the year 1791, by the Rev. Wm. Gilpin, vicar of Boldre, together with an account of the author, by himself, and a pedigree of the Gilpin family.* ed. William Jackson. *C.W.A.A.S., E.S.* **2**, 1879. Includes pedigree, 18-19th c.

Glaister

GLAISTER, JOHN. 'The Glaisters of Scotland and Cumberland', *C.W.A.A.S., Tr.* N.S. **20**, 1920, 188-231. Medieval-19th c., includes pedigree, 14-15th c., and list of wills, 1569-1761.

Graham

BAIN, JOSEPH. 'The Grahams or Graemes of the Debateable Land: their traditional origin considered', *Archaeological journal* **43**, 1886, 116-23.

GRAHAM, T.H.B. 'The Barony of Liddel and its occupants', *C.W.A.A.S., Tr.* N.S. **11**, 1911, 55-83. Includes pedigrees of Graham, 16-17th c.

G[RAHAM], T.H.B. 'The Grahams of Esk', *C.W.A.A.S., Tr.* N.S. **30**, 1930, 224-6. Includes pedigree of Graham of Brackenhill, 17-18th c.

REID, R.C. 'The Border Grahams: their origin and distribution', *Dumfriesshire and Galloway Natural History and Antiquarian Society transactions* 3rd series **38**, 1961, 85-113.

SPENCE, R.T. 'The Graham clans and lands on the eve of the Jacobean pacification', *C.W.A.A.S., Tr.* N.S. **80**, 1980, 79-102.

Family Histories etc. continued

Graves

GRAVES, F.R. 'Notes on the Graves family', *C.F.H.S.N.* **18**, 1981, 6-7. 18th c.

Greystoke

WILSON, JAMES. 'Some extinct Cumberland families, IV: the Greystokes', *Ancestor* **6**, 1903, 121-34. Includes pedigree, 12-16th c.
'The arms of Greystock', *Northern genealogist* **5**, 1902, 53.

Griffith

SHAVER, CHESTER L. 'The Griffith family: Wordsworth's kinsmen', *C.W.A.A.S., Tr.* N.S. **63**, 1963, 199-230. 17-19th c.

Grindal

See Sandwith and Winder

Guy

BIRLEY, ERIC. 'The Guys of Kendal and Watercrook', *C.W.A.A.S., Tr.* N.S. **58**, 1958, 94-105. 17-18th c., includes pedigree, and will of Henry Guy, 1708.
FAHY, T.G. 'The Guy family', *C.F.H.S.N.* **35**, 1985, 2-3. Includes pedigree, 17-18th c.

Gylby

See Fell

Haig

See Fell

Halden

HEDLEY, W. PERCY. 'The sons of Halden, lord of Catterlen', *C.W.A.A.S., Tr.* N.S. **64**, 1964, 98-109. 12th c.

Haltclough

See Burden

Hardy

HARDY, CHARLES FREDERIC. *The Hardys of Barbon, and some other Westmoreland statesmen: their kith, kin and childer.* Constable & Co., 1913. 16-19th c., including hearth tax returns for Middleton, Barbon and Casterton, 1670, and list of tenants of Barbon, 1718.

Hayston

HATSTON, J.B. 'The Hayston story', *C.F.H.S.N.* **17**, 1980, 2-4 & **18**, 1981, 7-9. 18-19th c., includes marriage extracts from Workington parish register.

Hewetson

WATSON, KEITH LOVET. *The Hewetsons of Ravenstonedale and North Westmorland.* [ ]: the author, 1965. Includes pedigrees, 16-20th c.

Heywood

See also Fell

Hill

BALLASIS, EDWARD. 'Hill of Crackenthorpe', *C.W.A.A.S., Tr.* **1**, 1876, 197-205. Includes tipped in pedigree, 16-19th c.
See also Fell

Hodgson

HODGSON, GEOFFREY MARTIN. *A Hodgson family.* Standon, Hertfordshire: the author, 1982. Includes pedigree, 17-20th c. Also of Yorkshire and Co.Durham.
HODGSON, JAMES. 'The Hodgsons of Bascodyke', *C.W.A.A.S., Tr.* N.S. **25**, 1925, 244-67. 16-18th c., includes wills.

Holmes

HUDLESTON, C. ROY. 'Kings of Mardale', *C.F.H.S.N.* **55**, 1990, 5-6. Holmes family, mainly 18-20th c.

Honywood

See Wastell

Huartson

BARKER, F.W. 'The indentures', *C.F.H.S.N.* **58**, 1991, 1-4. Includes pedigree of Huartson, Atkinson and Barker, 18-20th c.

Hudleston

COWPER, H.S. 'Millom Castle and the Hudlestons', *C.W.A.A.S., Tr.* N.S. **24**, 1924, 181-234. Includes pedigrees, 13-18th c.
JACKSON, W. 'The Hudlestons of Hutton John, the Hudlestons of Kelston, now of Hutton John, and the Hudlestons of Whitehaven', *C.W.A.A.S., Tr.* **11**, 1891, 433-65. Includes folded pedigrees, 17-19th c., with extracts from parish registers, wills, etc.
See also West

Hutton

GRAHAM, T.H.B. 'The Huttons of Cumberland', *C.W.A.A.S., Tr.* N.S. **30**, 1930, 68-88. Medieval-18th c., includes pedigrees.
PARKER, F.H.M. 'Inglewood Forest, part VII: The Huttons, hereditary foresters of Plumpton Hay; an account of the family and office from the reign of William Rufus to the reign of James I', *C.W.A.A.S., Tr.* N.S. **11**, 1911, 1-37.
See also Burdett

Ireby

IRBY, PAUL AUBERT. *The Irbys of Lincolnshire and the Irebys of Cumberland*. 3 vols. Reid Bros, 1938-9. Pt.1. The Irbys of Lincolnshire. Pt.2. The Irebys of Cumberland. Medieval-20th c. Includes folded pedigrees in separate case.

Irton

HASWELL, FRANCIS. 'The Irtons of Threlkeld', *C.W.A.A.S., Tr.* N.S. **24**, 1924, 17-28. 16-18th c. Includes will of Wilfred Irton, 1736.

TAYLOR, S. 'The Irtons of Irton Hall', *C.W.A.A.S., Tr.* N.S. **41**, 1941, 72-122. See also **76**, 1976, 220-21. 13-19th c., includes folded pedigrees, etc.

James

See also Radcliffe

Jefferson

BOUCH, C.M. LOWTHER. 'The Jeffersons of Westward', *C.W.A.A.S., Tr.* N.S. **41**, 1941, 181-96 & **42**, 1942, 103-11. Includes folded pedigree of Jefferson and Brisco, 16-20th c., wills, etc.

Kirkbride

GRAHAM, T.H.B. 'The Kirkbrides of Kirkbride', *C.W.A.A.S., Tr.* N.S. **15**, 1915, 63-75. Includes folded pedigree, medieval.

GRAHAM, T.H.B. 'Landed gentry', *C.W.A.A.S., Tr.* N.S. **32**, 1932, 45-56. Family histories of Kirkbride of Ellerton, Blennerhasset of Carlisle, and Scaife of Winton, including pedigrees, 14-17th c.

Kitchin

COWPER, H.S. 'Robert Kitchin, mayor of Bristol: a native of Kendal', *C.W.A.A.S., Tr.* N.S. **29**, 1929, 193-204. Includes pedigree, 15-17th c.

Knipe

H[UDLESTON], C. ROY. 'The Knipes of Flodder', *C.F.H.S.N.* **51**, 1989, 1-5. 18th c.

Lamplugh

JABEZ-SMITH, A.R. 'An interpolation in a Lamplugh parish register', *C.W.A.A.S., Tr.* N.S. **61**, 1961, 120-30. Lamplugh family, 17th c.

JABEZ-SMITH, A.R. 'The Lamplughs of Cockermouth and a Yorkshire inheritance', *C.W.A.A.S., Tr.* N.S. **6**, 1967, 81-92. Includes pedigree, 15-17th c.

Lamplugh *continued*

JABEZ-SMITH, A.R. 'Some portraits at Dovenby Hall', *C.W.A.A.S., Tr.* N.S. **64**, 1964, 256-63. Mainly of the Lamplugh family; includes pedigree, 16-18th c.

TAYLOR, S. 'The family of Lamplugh, of Lamplugh in Cumberland', *C.W.A.A.S., Tr.* N.S. **38**, 1938, 71-137 & **39**, 1939, 71-108. 12-20th c., includes pedigrees and wills, etc.

See also Pearson

Lancaster

RAGG, FREDERICK W. 'De Lancaster', *C.W.A.A.S., Tr.* N.S. **10**, 1910, 395-494 & 541-51. Medieval; includes folded pedigrees, deeds, inquisitions post mortem, etc.

WASHINGTON, GEORGE. 'The parentage of William de Lancaster, lord of Kendal', *C.W.A.A.S., Tr.* N.S. **62**, 1962, 95-100. 12-13th c., includes pedigree.

Lathom

WASHINGTON, GEORGE. 'Margaret de Lathom, or Lethom, wife of Walter de Strickland (1323-1407) of Sizergh', *C.W.A.A.S., Tr.* N.S. **63**, 1963, 170-77.

Law

JACKSON, WM. 'The Laws of Buck Crag in Cartmel, and of Bampton', *C.W.A.A.S., Tr.* **2**, 1876, 264-76. Cartmel, Lancashire; includes folded pedigree, 16-18th c., with wills.

LAW, SIR ALGERNON. 'Notes on the family of the Right Rev. Edmund Law, D.D.', *C.W.A.A.S., Tr.* N.S. **19**, 1919, 151-6. 18th c., includes biographical notes on the 13 children of Bishop Law.

LAW, R.C.E. 'The Law family', *C.F.H.S.N.* **42**, 1987, 10-12. 16-20th c.

NOBLE, MISS. 'The parentage of Bishop Law', *C.W.A.A.S., Tr.* N.S. **7**, 1907, 108-9. 17-18th c.

Lawson

MANDELL, SUSAN. 'Lawson family of Carlisle and Egremont', *C.F.H.S.N.* **62**, 1992, 5. Pedigree, 18-19th c.

Layburne

WIPER, WILLIAM. 'The Layburnes of Cunswick', *C.W.A.A.S., Tr.* **10**, 1889, 124-57. Includes folded pedigree, 14-18th c., deeds, wills, etc.

Layton

HUDLESTON, C. ROY. 'The last Laytons of Dalemain', *C.W.A.A.S., Tr.* N.S. **44**, 1944, 93-99. Includes pedigree, 17th c., and wills.

Family Histories etc. *continued*

Leathes

THOMPSON, B.L. 'The Leathes family of Dalehead', *C.W.A.A.S., Tr.* N.S. **60**, 1960, 109-19. 16-18th c., includes folded pedigree and three epitaphs.

Lengleys

RAGG, FREDERICK W. 'Lengleys: Asby Parva, Asby Cotesford and Highhead', *C.W.A.A.S., Tr.* N.S. **20**, 1920, 66-96. Includes medieval pedigrees, deeds, etc., and will of Sir Thomas Lengleys, 1362.

Lethom

See Lathom

Levington

GRAHAM, T.H.B. 'The de Levingtons of Kirklinton', *C.W.A.A.S., Tr.* N.S. **11**, 1911, 59-75. Medieval; includes pedigrees.

WILSON, JAMES. 'Some extinct Cumberland families, II: the Levingtons', *Ancestor* **3**, 1802, 80-84. 13th c. pedigree.

Lonsdale

See Fell

Losh

MCCULLOCH, M. 'The Losh family of Woodside', *C.F.H.S.N.* **53**, 1989, 1-2. 18-19th c.

Lowther

BEWLEY, EDMUND T. 'Some notes on the Lowthers who held judicial office in Ireland in the seventeenth century', *C.W.A.A.S., Tr.* N.S. **2**, 1902, 1-28.

BOUCH, C.M. LOWTHER. 'The descendants of William Lowther of the Rose', *C.W.A.A.S., Tr.* N.S. **39**, 1939, 109-35. 15-17th c., includes pedigree and wills, etc.

BOUCH, C.M. LOWTHER. 'Lowther of Colby Leathes', *C.W.A.A.S., Tr.* N.S. **24**, 1924, 117-35.

BOUCH, C.M. LOWTHER. 'The origins and early pedigree of the Lowther family', *C.W.A.A.S., Tr.* N.S. **48**, 1948, 114-24. 13-16th c.

HAINSWORTH, D.R. 'The Lowther younger sons: a seventeenth century case study', *C.W.A.A.S., Tr.* N.S. **88**, 1988, 149-60. Includes pedigree, 16-18th c.

OWEN, HUGH. *The Lowther family: eight hundred years of a family of ancient gentry and worship.* Chichester: Phillimore, 1990. Of Carlisle, Ingleton, Whitehaven, Marske, Yorkshire, Holker, Lancashire, Swillington, Yorkshire, etc. Includes pedigrees, 12-20th c.

Lowther *continued*

PARKER, F.H.M. 'The marriage of Sir Hugh de Louthre and Margaret de Whale', *C.W.A.A.S., Tr.* N.S. **2**, 1902, 151-4. Lowther family; 14th c.

RAGG, FREDERICK W. 'Early Lowther and de Louther', *C.W.A.A.S., Tr.* N.S. **16**, 1916, 108-68. Includes folded pedigrees, 12-16th c., and deeds.

Lumley

BEASTALL, T.W. *A North Country estate: the Lumleys and Saundersons as landowners, 1600-1900.* Phillimore, 1975.

Machell

BELLASIS, E. 'Machell of Crackenthorpe', *C.W.A.A.S., Tr.* **8**, 1886, 416-66. Includes folded pedigrees, 12-19th c., wills, parish register extracts, etc.

CRESSWELL, LIONEL. 'Crackenthorpe: its manor, hall and the Machell family', *C.W.A.A.S., Tr.* N.S. **33**, 1933, 113-32. 12-19th c.

HUDLESTON, C. ROY. 'Thomas Machell, his wife and children, and his Whelpdale stepchildren', *C.W.A.A.S., Tr.* N.S. **70**, 1970, 110-45. 17th c., includes wills.

Mandell

'Some Mandells in West Cumberland', *C.F.H.S.N.* **10**, 1979, 6-10. 18-19th c.

Mann

'Mann memoranda', *C.F.H.S.N.* **54**, 1990, 3-6. 18-19th c.

Matthews

DIXON, PHILIP. 'Paddock Hole: a Cumberland house with a lower-end parlour', *C.W.A.A.S., Tr.* N.S. **71**, 1971, 139-50. Includes pedigree of Matthews, 17-19th c.

Miers

HUDLESTON, CHRISTOPHE ROY. 'A Cumberland will', *Notes & queries* **93**, 1948, 31-3. Note on Thomasin and Thomas Miers, beneficiaries of will of Thomas Whelpdale, 1756-71.

Milborne

WHITE, E.A. 'Milborne family', *Miscellanea genealogica et heraldica* 2nd series **2**, 1888, 154-5. Reprinted in *C.F.H.S.N.* **36**, 1985, 11-12. 16th c. notes in a book of hours.

Millican

MILLICAN, G.T. 'Nichol Forest and Stapleton', *C.F.H.S.N.* **18**, 1981, 4-6. Millican or Milliken family, 18-19th c.

Moor

MOOR, C. *Erminois: a book of family records.*
Kendal: Titus Wilson, 1918. Moor family,
medieval-20th c. with notes on many associated
families.

Morton

GODWIN, JEREMY. 'The Mortons', *C.F.H.S.N.* **44**,
1987, 3-6. 18-19th c.

Mounsey

LEWIS, O.B. 'The Mounseys of Patterdale',
C.F.H.S.N. **5**, 1977, 1-3. 17-19th c.

Mulcaster

GRAHAM, T.H.B. 'The family of de Mulcaster',
C.W.A.A.S., Tr. N.S. **18**, 1918, 110-24.
13-17th c., includes brief pedigrees.

Musgrave

MUSGRAVE, PERCY. *Notes on the ancient family of
Musgrave, of Musgrave, Westmorland, and its
various branches in Cumberland, Yorkshire,
Northumberland, Somerset, &c., compiled
mainly from original sources.* Leeds: privately
printed, 1911.
See also Warcope

Neave

See Atkinson

Nelson

NELSON, N. 'A Cumbrian and family in America',
C.F.H.S.N. **17**, 1980, 1-2. Nelson family, 18th c.
WATSON, GEORGE. 'The Nelsons of Penrith',
C.W.A.A.S., Tr. N.S. **1**, 1901, 104-113. See also
9, 1909, 331-2. 17-19th c.

Neville

See Strickland

Noble

See Fell

Orfeur

JACKSON, WILLIAM. 'The Orfeurs of High Close,
Plumbland', *C.W.A.A.S., Tr.* **3**, 1878, 99-126.
Includes folded pedigree, 14-19th c., wills and
parish register extracts, etc.

Osmotherley

SKELTON, JOSEPH. 'The Osmotherleys of
Cumberland', *C.W.A.A.S., Tr.* N.S. **16**, 1916,
169-204. 13-20th c., includes pedigree, extracts
from parish registers, list of wills, etc.

Parke

See Romney

Parker

PARKER, F.H.M. 'The Parkers of Old Town, with
some notes on the Branthwaites of Carlingill
and the Birkbecks of Orton Hall', *C.W.A.A.S.,
Tr.* **15**, 1900, 104-16. Includes folded pedigree,
17-19th c.
See also Webster

Parr

DUCKETT, SIR GEORGE. 'The Parrs of Kendal
Castle', *C.W.A.A.S., Tr.* **2**, 1876, 186-96.
Includes medieval pedigree.
P., H. 'Early pedigrees of the Parr family',
Topographer and genealogist **3**, 1858, 352-60.
See also 597-8. Pedigree, 14-16th c.

Patrickson

FAHY, T.G. 'The Patricksons of Ennerdale',
C.W.A.A.S., Tr. N.S. **66**, 1966, 470-73. Extract
from a Chancery suit, with pedigree, 17-18th c.
LITTLEDAL, RALPH P. 'Some notes on the
Patricksons of Ennerdale', *C.W.A.A.S., Tr.* N.S.
25, 1925, 128-243. 14-18th c., includes folded
pedigrees.

Pearson

JABEZ-SMITH, A.R. 'Anthony Pearson, an early
Cumbrian Quaker', *C.W.A.A.S., Tr.* N.S. **84**,
1984, 99-102. Includes pedigree, 16-18th c.,
showing relationship to Lamplugh family, and
will, 1665 (which describes him as 'of
Durham').

Peile

'Ten generations in Lakeland', *C.F.H.S.N.* **33**,
1984, 6-8. Peile family, 18-20th c.

Peill

BARNES, MARGARET. 'The Peill missionaries',
C.F.H.S.N. **18**, 1981, 3-4. Includes pedigree, 18-
19th c.

Pennington

See Askew

Penruddock

NOBLE, ARTHUR H. *The Penruddock family: the
genealogical & historical account of the
Penruddock families of Cumberland &
Wiltshire, with a pedigree of 17 generations
from about 1400 to present day.* [ ]: A.H. Noble,
1968. Duplicated typescript.

Percy

CLARK, GEO. T. 'The house of Percy, entitled
Barons Lucy of Cockermouth', *C.W.A.A.S., Tr.*
11, 1891, 399-432.

Family Histories etc. *continued*

Philipson
DARLOW, G.S. 'A Philipson family prayer book', *C.W.A.A.S., Tr.* N.S. **59**, 1959, 105-14. 17th c.

FAHY, T.G. 'The Philipson family', *C.W.A.A.S., Tr.* N.S. **64**, 1964, 150-213 & **73**, 1973, 226-81. See also **85**, 1985, 268-9. Includes pedigree, 15-18th c., probate records, etc.

Porter
PARKER, C.A. 'A pedigree of the family of Porter of Bolton, Cumberland', *C.W.A.A.S., Tr.* N.S. **14**, 1914, 83-131. 15-19th c.

Postlethwayt
HARTSHORNE, ALBERT. 'Notes on the Postlethwayts of Millom, with reference to an initialled spoon of that family', *C.W.A.A.S., Tr.* **10**, 1889, 244-52. Includes folded pedigree, 16-19th c.

Radcliffe
EVANS, MARGARET, ed. *Letters of Richard Radcliffe and John James of Queen's College, Oxford, 1755-83.* Oxford Historical Society **9**, 1888. Includes folded pedigree of Radcliffe and James, 18-19th c., Cumberland families.

See also Derwentwater

Ransford
RANSFORD, ALFRED. *The origin of the Ransfords, from the baronial settlement in England, temp Doomsday (1086) and their immediate descendants.* Mitchell Hughes & Clarke, 1919. Includes pedigree, 11-13th c.

Ransome
See Atkinson

Raughton
See Burden

Rawes
'The Rawes family', *C.F.H.S.N.* **4**, 1990, 1-3. 18-19th c.

Ray
SWIFT, F.B. 'Rays and Glaisters of Wigton', *C.F.H.S.N.* **22**, 1982, 5-6. 18-19th c.

Redman
GREENWOOD, W. 'The Redmans of Levens', *C.W.A.A.S., Tr.* N.S. **3**, 1903, 272-306. Includes medieval pedigrees (one folded).

GREENWOOD, W. 'The Redmaynes of Levens', *Northern genealogist* **5**, 1902, 2-12. Medieval.

GREENWOOD, W. 'Further notes on early Redman history', *Northern genealogist* **6**, 1903, 3-6.

Restwold
See Skelton

Richmond
CHIPPINDALL, W.H. 'On the family of de Richmond, constables on Richmond Castle, and their connection with Corby', *C.W.A.A.S., Tr.* N.S. **16**, 1916, 97-9.

JACKSON, WILLIAM. 'The Richmonds of Highhead', *C.W.A.A.S., Tr.* **2**, 1876, 108-47. Includes folded pedigrees, 16-19th c., with extracts from parish registers and wills, etc.

See also Simpson

Robinson
HUDLESTON, C. ROY. 'Robinson of Kendal', *C.W.A.A.S., Tr.* N.S. **63**, 1963, 291-2. 18th c.

ROBINSON, JOHN. 'The connection of a Kendal family with Rokeby', *C.W.A.A.S., Tr.* N.S. **6**, 1906, 171-2. Robinson family, 18-19th c. Rokeby, Yorkshire.

Romney
POSTLETHWAITE, T.N. 'George Romney: some notes on his ancestry', *C.W.A.A.S., Tr.* N.S. **26**, 1926, 349-77. Descent from the Parke family; includes pedigrees, 17-18th c., and wills of Parke family, etc.

Rook
'A search for some missing Rooks', *C.F.H.S.N.* **9**, 1978, 4-7. Includes many extracts from 18-19th c. registers and census returns.

See also Atkinson

Routledge
HARRISON, J.V. 'The Routledges of Cumcrook', *C.W.A.A.S., Tr.* N.S. **65**, 1965, 320-70. See also **66**, 1966, 477. Includes folded pedigrees, 17-19th c., of Routledge, Sowerby, Wallace and Thompson, with probate records.

See also Brown

Salkeld
MOORE, J. GRANGE. *Salkelds through seven centuries.* Phillimore, 1988. Cumberland, Yorkshire, Suffolk, Shropshire and Cheshire; includes pedigrees, probate records, etc.

SALKELD, R.E. 'An over-looked marriage', *C.F.H.S.N.* **53**, 1989, 11-14. Includes pedigree of Salkeld of Cumberland and Northumberland, 16th c.

Sandford

BOUCH, C.M. LOWTHER. 'An account of some litigation about Askham Hall begun in 1775', *C.W.A.A.S., Tr.* N.S. **43**, 1943, 137-46. Discusses litigation concerning the will of William Sandford, 1730; includes pedigree.

RAGG, FREDERICK W. 'Helton Flechan, Askham, and Sandford of Askham', *C.W.A.A.S., Tr.* N.S. **21**, 1921, 174-233. Includes pedigree, medieval-18th c., inquisitions post mortem, wills, etc.

Sands

'Extracts from the parish registers of Saint Bees, relating to the family of Sands', *Miscellanea genealogica et heraldica* N.S. **4**, 1884, 59-60.

Sandwith

THOMPSON, W.N. 'A Sandwith-Grindal pedigree', *C.W.A.A.S., Tr.* N.S. **5**, 1905, 68-71. From the visitation of Lincolnshire, 1654.

Sandys

SANDYS, E.S. *History of the family of Sandys of Cumberland, afterwards of Furness in North Lancashire, and its branches in other parts of England and in Ireland.* 2 vols. Barrow Printing Co., 1930. Includes pedigrees, 13-19th c., (in Vol.2), also index of marriages, etc.

WILSON, JAMES. 'The arms of the Sandys of Cumberland', *Ancestor* 3, 1902, 85. 16th c.

Saunderson

See Lowther

Scaife

SCAIFE, M.M.R.C. *The Scaife family: notes historical and traditional.* Exeter: William Pollard, 1925. Includes pedigree, 17th c.

See also Kirkbride

Senhouse

SENHOUSE, R.M. LE F. 'Senhouse of Seascale Hall, in Cumberland', *C.W.A.A.S., Tr.* **12**, 1893, 247-60. Medieval-19th c.

Sessions

See Atkinson

Sewell

MANDELL, SUSAN. 'Some Sewells', *C.F.H.S.N.* **21**, 1981, 6-11. Extracts from 18-19th c. bishops' transcripts and censuses, etc.

Shortridge

JOLLY, M. AIRD. 'The Shortridges: the records of a Cumberland family', *C.W.A.A.S., Tr.* N.S. **39**, 1939, 35-44. 17-19th c.

Simpson

DAVIDSON, E. *The Simpsons of Kendal: craftsmen in wood, 1885-1952.* [Lancaster]: University of Lancaster Visual Arts Centre, 1978.

SWIFT, F.B. 'Orthwaite Hall and the families of Simpson, Richmond and Browne', *C.W.A.A.S., Tr.* N.S. **69**, 1969, 221-39 & **70**, 1970, 146-60. Includes wills, with a 17-18th c. pedigree of Simpson.

Sinclair

See Atkinson

Sizergh

HUNT, JOHN G. 'The wives of Walter Sizergh of Strickland', *New York historical and genealogical register* **114**, 1960, 51-8.

Skelton

GRAHAM, T.H.B. 'The Skeltons of Skelton', *C.W.A.A.S., Tr.* N.S. **33**, 1933, 34-42. 14th c.

PARKER, F.H.M. 'The development of Inglewood, and an account of the Skeltons of Armathwaite and the Restwolds of High Head', *C.W.A.A.S., Tr.* N.S. **12**, 1912, 1-28. Includes pedigree, 14-16th c.

Somerford

See Atkinson

Southayk

See Burden

Stanley

See Atkinson

Stephenson

HUDLESTON, C. ROY. 'The Stephensons of Nentsberry, Alston', *C.W.A.A.S., Tr.* N.S. **70**, 1970, 281-2. Includes pedigree, 18-20th c.

Stirkland

See Burden

Strickland

BELLASIS, E. 'Strickland of Sizergh', *C.W.A.A.S., Tr.* **10**, 1889, 75-94. Includes folded pedigree, 13-19th c.

HORNYOLD-STRICKLAND, HENRY. 'The wives of Walter Strickland', *C.W.A.A.S., Tr.* N.S. **61**, 1961, 104-11. 16th c.

SCOTT, DANIEL. *The Stricklands of Sizergh Castle: the records of twenty-five generations of a Westmorland family.* Kendal: Titus Wilson, 1908.

STRICKLAND, EDELINE. *Sizergh Castle, Westmorland, and notes on twenty-five generations of the Strickland family.* Kendal: Titus Wilson, 1898.

Warcope

MISTLETOE. 'Digest of old cases referring to the families of Warcope, Musgrave and Warde and to the county of Westmorland', *Northern notes and queries* **1**, 1906, 166-7. 16-17th c.

Warde

See Warcope

Waring

See Atkinson

Washington

HARPER, W.S. 'Whitehaven and the Washington family', *C.W.A.A.S., Tr.* **5**, 1881, 98-108. 17th c.

HEDLEY, W. PERCY, & WASHINGTON, GEORGE. 'The Washingtons of Helton Flecket, Westmorland', *C.W.A.A.S., Tr.* N.S. **68**, 1968, 42-56. Includes pedigree, 13-14th c.

HINCHCLIFFE, E. 'The Washingtons at Whitehaven and Appleby', *C.W.A.A.S., Tr.* N.S. **71**, 1971, 151-98. See also **72**, 1972, 336-7. 17-18th c. Includes pedigree of Gale, 17-18th c., will of Mildred Gale, 1701, and notes on the Deane family.

PEARSON, ALEXANDER. 'The Westmorland and Lancashire Washingtons', in *The doings of a country solicitor.* Kendal: Titus Wilson & Son, 1947, 152-67.

SMITH, J.C.C. 'New notes on the ancestry of George Washington', *C.W.A.A.S., Tr.* **9**, 1888, 97-100. Includes pedigree of Gale, 18th c.

Wastell

PARKER, F.H.M. 'The pedigree of Wastell of Wastell Head, with a memoir of General Honywood of Howgill Castle', *C.W.A.A.S., Tr.* N.S. **1**, 1901, 147-54. Includes folded pedigree, 16-19th c.

Waugh

WAGNER, HENRY. 'A pedigree of the descendants of John Waugh, D.D., showing their connection with the family of Tullie of Carlisle', *C.W.A.A.S., Tr.* **13**, 1895, 440-8. 17-18th c. Includes will of John Waugh, 1765.

Webster

DUKE, JOAN E. 'A young lady's letters', *C.F.H.S.N.* **55**, 1990, 1-4. 19th c. letters, with a pedigree showing relationship of Webster and Parker, 18-19th c.

West

HUDLESTON, C. ROY. 'The marriage of Charles West and Mary Hudleston in 1677', *C.W.A.A.S., Tr.* N.S. **27**, 1927, 164-9.

Wharton

BAIN, JOSEPH. 'The Lords Wharton and their shield', *Genealogist* N.S. **8**, 1892, 6-7. See also 127-9. 14-16th c.

SIMPSON, DR. 'Wharton Hall and the Wharton family', *C.W.A.A.S., Tr.* **1**, 1874, 224-37. 16-17th c.

Whelpdale

HASWELL, FRANCIS. 'The Whelpdale family of Penrith', *C.W.A.A.S., Tr.* N.S. **43**, 1943, 31-49. Includes pedigrees, 16-19th c., and wills. See also Machell and Miers

White

DEARDEN, J. 'White of Alston and Carrigill', *C.F.H.S.N.* **45**, 1987, 8-9. Pedigree, 18-19th c.

Wigton

WILSON, JAMES. 'Some extinct Cumberland families, I: the Wigtons', *Ancestor* **3**, 1902, 73-80. Pedigree, 12-14th c.

Wilkinson

SWIFT, F.B. 'Eelchist: a forgotten farm in Holm Cultram', *C.W.A.A.S., Tr.* N.S. **51**, 1951, 108-16. Gives descent in the Wilkinson family, 17-18th c., with wills.

Williamson

SACHSE, K.H. 'The Williamsons', *C.F.H.S.N.* **35**, 1985, 6-8. 18-19th c.

Wilson

BROWN, R. PERCIVAL. *Edward Wilson of Nether Levens (1557-1653) and his kin. C.W.A.A.S., T.S.* **12**, 1930. Includes folded pedigrees, 16-19th c.

FOSTER, JOSEPH. *The pedigree of Wilson of High Wray and Kendal and the families connected with them.* Head, Hole & Co., 1871. High Wray, Lancashire. 17-19th c., includes list of 'matches'.

SOMERVELL, JOHN. *Isaac and Rachel Wilson, Quakers of Kendal, 1714-1785.* Swarthmore Press, 1924. Includes genealogical notes, 17-19th c.

'Wilson of Dallam', *C.F.H.S.N.* **48**, 1988, 1-2. 19th c.

Family Histories etc. continued

Winder

WINDER, F.A. 'The Winders of Lorton', *C.W.A.A.S., Tr.* **12**, 1893, 439-57. See also **14**, 1897, 198-207. Includes pedigree, 18th c., extracts from parish registers, wills, etc.

WINDER, F.A. 'Further notes on the Winders of Lorton', *C.W.A.A.S., Tr.* **15**, 1899, 229-38. Includes pedigree of Grindal of St.Bees, showing connection with Woodhall, Dacre, and Wyberg families; 16th c.

Windesore

See Duckett

Woodhall

See Winder

Wordsworth

See Griffith

Wren

JARMAN, L.C. 'The Wren family', *C.F.H.S.N.* **58**, 1991, 5-7. Includes 18th c. pedigree and parish register abstracts.

Wyberg

FAIR, MARY C. 'The family of Wyberg of Clifton', *C.W.A.A.S., Tr.* N.S. **49**, 1949, 221-2. Brief note; medieval.

See also Engayne and Winder

Wykeham

See Atkinson

7. PARISH REGISTERS AND OTHER RECORDS OF BIRTHS, MARRIAGES AND DEATHS

The importance of parish registers to the genealogist cannot be over-stated; they are normally one of the first sources to be consulted. The Cumbrian researcher is fortunate, since many Cumberland and Westmorland registers have been published: they are listed below. It may still, however, be necessary to check the originals. A guide to these is currently in preparation, and will be published as the Cumbrian volume of the *National index to parish registers*. Until this is in print, reliance must be placed on the now rather out-dated:

SWIFT, F.B. 'The parish registers of Cumberland, Westmorland, and Lancashire North-of-the Sands', *C.W.A.A.S., Tr.* N.S. **56**, 1956, 144-54. Includes lists of unpublished transcripts, as well as published material—the latter is superseded by the present work.

Reference may also be made to:

JONES, G.P. 'Baptisms and burials in twenty northern parishes', *C.W.A.A.S., Tr.* N.S. **74**, 1974, 109-17. Based on parish registers.

WHITEHEAD, HENRY. 'Westmorland parish registers', *C.W.A.A.S., Tr.* **13**, 1895, 125-41.

WHITEHEAD, H. 'The transcripts of the registers in Brampton Deanery', *C.W.A.A.S., Tr.* **5**, 1881, 261-51. General discussion.

WHITEHEAD, H. 'Cumberland parish registers, no.1: Brampton Deanery', *C.W.A.A.S., Tr.* **14**, 1897, 212-43. Detailed list with extensive notes.

An important project to index Westmorland parish registers is described in:

SMITH, SYDNEY G. 'The Westmorland and North Lancashire marriage index', *C.F.H.S.N.* **18**, 1981, 13-14.

One of the major problems genealogists have to deal with is tracing ancestors' movements across parish boundaries. Most family history societies include listings of 'strays' in their journals; the Cumbria Family History Society goes one better by publishing a full index every few years:

CUMBRIA FAMILY HISTORY SOCIETY. *Strays.* Manchester: Cumbria Family History Society, 1979-. Irregular.

See also:

COOKSON, EDWARD. 'Waifs and strays', *Northern notes and queries* **1**, 1906, 153-4, 168-9, 209 & 244. Extracts from Yorkshire parish registers relating to the four northern counties.

Parish Registers etc. continued

Marriage bonds provide a useful supplement to parish registers. Those for the deaneries of the former Archdeaconry of Richmond—Copeland in Cumberland, Kendal and Lonsdale in Westmorland—are noted in:

Marriage bonds for the deaneries of Lonsdale, Kendal, Furness, and Copeland, part of the Archdeaconry of Richmond, now preserved at Lancaster. Lancashire & Cheshire Record Society **74-5, 80-81, 83, 100 & 115**, 1920-75. Pt.1. 1648-1710. Pt.2. 1711-22. Pt.3. 1723-8. Pt.4. 1729-34. Pt.5. 1734-8. Pt.6. 1739-45. Title varies; the documents are now at Preston, and include bonds for the Deanery of Amounderness, Lancashire.

Brief extracts only have been published from other ecclesiastical jurisdictions:

HARRISON, BRETT. 'Cumbrian marriage bonds', *C.F.H.S.N.* **38**, 1986, 6-7. From Ripon Diocesan records, 1628-98.

HOWE, J.J. 'Marriage bonds', *Northern notes and queries* **1**, 1906, 5-6, 41-2 & 83-4. At Carlisle, 1743-8, and Durham, 1666. Not completed.

'Carlisle marriage bonds', *C.F.H.S.N.* **12**, 1979, 6. For February and March 1796 only.

'Carlisle marriage bonds', *C.F.H.S.N.* **28**, 1983, 23-4. For 1816.

Notices of births, marriages and deaths frequently appear in newspapers. Many of these notices have been reprinted by the Cumbria Family History Society and other publishers, and are listed here in chronological order:

GORDON, JOHN. *Border annals*. Annan: G. Gilchrist, 1971. 18-19th c. births, marriages and deaths from a variety of North Cumberland newspapers and parish registers.

'Extracts from the *Athenaeum* relating to Cumberland', *C.F.H.S.N.* **34**, 1985, 19-20; **36**, 1985, 12-13. Births, marriages and deaths, 1807.

'From the *Cumberland Pacquet*', *C.F.H.S.N.* **39**, 1985, 13. Marriages and burials, 1814 and 1820.

'From the *Lancaster Gazette*', *C.F.H.S.N.* **40**, 1986, 4-6. Marriages and deaths, 1827-9, mainly in Westmorland.

'From the *Westmorland Gazette* November 14th 1835', *C.F.H.S.N.* **29**, 1983, 22-3. Marriages.

'From the *Westmorland Gazette* 12 March 1836', *C.F.H.S.N.* **30**, 1984, 25-7. Births, marriages and deaths; also for 26.12.1836.

HAYHURST, K. 'From the *Lancaster Gazette*', *C.F.H.S.N.* **49**, 1988, 16-18. Birth, marriage and death notices, 1836.

HAYHURST, KATH. 'Births, marriages and deaths in South Westmorland: *Lancaster Gazette* (1841)', *C.F.H.S.N.* **62**, 1992, 9-11.

'Marriages from the *Carlisle journal* May 1848', *C.F.H.S.N.* **28**, 1983, 24-6.

WRIGHT, M. 'Extracts from the *Kendal Mercury and Northern Advertiser* of Saturday 19 May 1849', *C.F.H.S.N.* **34**, 1985, 20-22.

'Cumbria-Liverpool', *C.F.H.S.N.* **45**, 1987, 7-8. Marriages from the *Cumberland Pacquet*, 1872-7.

ARNISON, JANET. 'Marriages from the *Penrith Herald* 1875', *C.F.H.S.N.* **38**, 1985, 15-16.

Alston

See Garrigill

Appleby

'Marriages at St.Michael's, Appleby', *C.F.H.S.N.* **11**, 1979, 17-18 & **12**, 1979, 10. 1665-90.

'Extra-parochial records', *C.F.H.S.N.* **31**, 1984, 22-3. Records of Appleby Grammar School, listing couples paying 'wedding money', 1729-90.

Asby

The Asby church register. Adlard & Son, 1894. An index rather than a transcript. Covers from 1657 to 1798; includes list of rectors.

Askham

NOBLE, MARY E. *The registers of the parish of Askham in the county of Westmoreland from 1566 to 1812.* Bemrose & Sons, 1904. Includes list of vicars. See also: NOBLE, MISS. 'A sketch of the church of Askham, and some account of the early parish registers', *C.W.A.A.S., Tr.* N.S. **4**, 1904, 92-103. Includes some extracts from the parish register, with list of vicars, 1346-1889.

Bampton

NOBLE, MARY E., ed. *Register of births, deaths and marriages of the parish of Bampton in the county of Westmoreland from 1637 to 1812.* Kendal: T. Wilson, 1897.

Barton

BRIERLY, HENRY, ed. *The registers of the parish church of Barton, Westmorland. Baptisms and marriages, 1666-1812. Burials, 1666-1830.* C.W.A.A.S., P.R.S. **5**, 1917. Includes list of clergy officiating at marriages, 1754-1812.

Bassenthwaite

SWIFT, F.B. 'The oldest parish registers of Bassenthwaite', *C.W.A.A.S., Tr.* N.S. **66**, 1966, 276-92. Description, with some 16-17th c. extracts, and will of Simon Bell, 1578.

Beaumont

'Marriages at Beaumont', *C.F.H.S.N.* **12**, 1979, 10-11. 1674-1708.

Bolton

HASWELL, FRANCIS. *The parish registers of Bolton, 1647-1812. C.W.A.A.S., P.R.S.* **32**. Penrith: the Society, 1944.

Bridekirk

BROWNE, WILLIAM. 'Bridekirk and its registers', *C.W.A.A.S., Tr.* **4**, 1880, 257-79. General discussion, with extracts relating to Lamplugh, Bromfield, Hutton, Tolson, Fletcher, Partis, Senhouse and other families.
HASWELL, J.F., ed. *The registers of Bridekirk, 1584-1812. C.W.A.A.S., P.R.S.* **14**, 1927. Includes list of vicars, 1307-1881.

Brough

BRIERLY, HENRY, ed. *The registers of Brough under Stainmore.* 2 vols. *C.W.A.A.S., P.R.S.* **9-10**, 1923-4. Pt.1. 1556-1706. Pt.2. 1706-1812.
'Baptisms at Brough-under-Stainmore', *C.F.H.S.N.* **30**, 1984, 12-13. Strays, 16-19th c.
'Brough registers: extracts: baptisms, 1813-26', *C.F.H.S.N.* **37**, 1985, 5.

Brougham

HASWELL, J.F., ed. *The registers of Brougham, 1645-1812. C.W.A.A.S., P.R.S.* **31**. Penrith: the Society, 1943.

Caldbeck

GOODWIN, ELLEN K. 'Caldbeck parish registers', *C.W.A.A.S., Tr.* **9**, 1888, 1-13. General discussion, including extracts, especially relating to Hutton, Vaux, Brownrigg and Salkeld families; 17-18th c.

Carlisle

FERGUSON, R.S. 'The parish registers of St.Mary's and St.Cuthbert's churches, Carlisle', *C.W.A.A.S., Tr.* **2**, 1876, 347-54. General discussion.

Cliburn

HASWELL, J.F., ed. *The registers of Cliburn, 1565-1812. C.W.A.A.S., P.R.S.* **20**, 1932. Includes list of rectors, 1284-1921.

Cockermouth

LEWIS, W. 'Baptismal register, 1651-1700: Congregational Church', in *Cockermouth miscellany.* C.F.H.S., [1987?].
REED, ELSIE. 'Births, marriages and deaths', in *Cockermouth miscellany.* C.F.H.S., [1987?].

Cockermouth *continued*

'Independent Chapel, Cockermouth, ref C107/150, P.R.O., London', *C.F.H.S.N.* **32**, 1984, 18. List of adult baptism, 1740-57.

Crosby Garrett

HASWELL, FRANCIS, ed. *The parish registers of Crosby Garrett, 1559-1812. C.W.A.A.S., P.R.S.* **33**. Penrith: the Society, 1945.

Crosby on Eden

HODGSON, T. HESKETH. 'Notes on the parish registers of Crosby-on-Eden', *C.W.A.A.S., Tr.*, **9**, 1888, 359-65. General discussion.
HODGSON, T.H., ed. 'Marriages at Crosby-on-Eden, 1665 to 1837', in PHILLIMORE, W.P.W., & RUSTON-HARRISON, C.W., eds. *C.P.R.M.* **2**, *P.P.R.S.* **166**. Phillimore, 1912, 57-78.

Crosby Ravensworth

HASWELL, J.F., ed. *The parish registers of Crosby Ravensworth, 1568-1812. C.W.A.A.S., P.R.S.* **25**, 1937.

Crosthwaite

BRIERLY, HENRY, & HASWELL, FRANCIS, eds. *The registers of Crosthwaite.* 4 vols. *C.W.A.A.S., P.R.S.* **16-19**, 1928-31. Vol.1. 1561-1600 (includes list of vicars, 1294-1917). Vol.2. 1600-1670. Vol.3. Baptisms and marriages, 1670-1812. Vol.4. Deaths, 1670-1812.
CROSTHWAITE, J. FISHER. 'The Crosthwaite registers', *C.W.A.A.S., Tr.* **2**, 1876, 225-41. General discussion, with extracts.
'The registers of Crosthwaite', *C.F.H.S.N.* **4**, 1977, 18-19. Marriages for 1567 only.
'Church magazine of Crosthwaite and St.John, Keswick', *C.F.H.S.N.* **36**, 1985, 7-8. Marriages, 1883-5 and 1893.

Crosthwaite cum Lyth

HASWELL, J.F., ed. *Registers of Crosthwaite-cum-Lyth, 1569-1812. C.W.A.A.S., P.R.S.* **23**, 1935. Includes list of curates, 1572-1925.

Dacre

BRIERLY, HENRY, ed. *The registers of the parish church of Dacre, Cumberland, 1559-1716. C.W.A.A.S., P.R.S.* **1**, 1912. Includes lists of clergy, 1296-1896.

Dalston

KUPER, M.E. 'Seven volumes of Dalston parish registers', *C.W.A.A.S., Tr.* **7**, 1884, 156-220. General discussion rather than a transcript, but includes many extracts, especially relating to the families of Dalston, Denton, Brisco, and Lowther.

WILSON, JAMES, ed. *The parish registers of Dalston, Cumberland.* 2 vols. Dalston: William R. Beck, 1893-5. v.1. 1570-1678. v.2. 1679-1812.

WILSON, JAMES. 'The Dalston transcript of 1589-90', *C.W.A.A.S., Tr.* **11**, 1891, 238-49. General discussion, without extracts.

Dean

SHERWEN, W. 'The registers of the parish of Dean, Cumberland', *C.W.A.A.S., Tr.* **4**, 1880, 96-107. General discussion.

'Marriages at Dean from B.T.'s', *C.F.H.S.N.* **30**, 1984, 27. 1689-1703/4.

Edmond Castle

GRAHAM, T.H.B. 'The old village of Edmond Castle', *C.W.A.A.S., Tr.* N.S. **8**, 1908, 13-30. Includes extracts from the parish registers of Hayton, 17-18th c., notes on deeds, 17-19th c., pedigree of Graham, etc.

Garrigill

CAINE, CEASAR, ed. *Garrigill, St.Johns church (chapel of ease to St.Augustine's, Alston): the register (baptisms, marriages and deaths) from 1699 to 1730.* Haltwhistle: R.M. Saint, 1901.

Gosforth

PARKER, CHAS. A. 'Gosforth registers', *C.W.A.A.S., Tr.* **8**, 1886, 70-81. General discussion with some extracts, including entries for the Senhouse family.

PARKER, CHARLES A., ed. 'Marriages at Gosforth, 1571 to 1837', in PHILLIMORE, W.P.W., & RUSTON-HARRISON, C.W., eds. *C.P.R.M.* **2**, *P.P.R.S.* **166**. Phillimore, 1912, 119-57.

Grasmere

JENNINGS, N.A. 'Old occupations', *Family Tree Magazine* **6**(1), 1989, 4-5. From Grasmere baptismal registers, 1812-1900.

'Grasmere marriages, 1813-1818', *C.F.H.S.N.* **34**, 1985, 25-6.

Great Orton

GILBANKS, W.F. 'The registers of Great Orton, Carlisle, 1568 to 1812', *C.W.A.A.S., Tr.* **8**, 1886, 245-56. General discussion.

GILBANKS, W.F., ed. *The registers of the parish church of St.Giles, Great Orton, Cumberland, 1568-1812. C.W.A.A.S., P.R.S.* **4**, 1915. Includes list of clergy officiating at marriages.

Greystoke

LEES, T. 'Extracts from the registers at Greystoke church during the reigns of Elizabeth and the Stuart Kings', *C.W.A.A.S., Tr.* **1**, 1874, 336-46. General discussion.

MACLEAN, ALLAN M., ed. *The registers of the parish of Greystoke in the county of Cumberland: baptisms, marriages and burials, 1559-1757.* Kendal: Titus Wilson, 1911. Includes brief notes on clergy.

Harrington

CURWEN, PATRICIA, ed. 'Marriages at Harrington, 1652 to 1837', in PHILLIMORE, W.P.W., & RUSTON-HARRISON, C.W., eds. *C.P.R.M.* **2**, *P.P.R.S.* **166**. Phillimore, 1912, 79-117.

Hayton

'Hayton, Cumbria', *C.F.H.S.N.* **35**, 1985, 10-14. Baptisms, marriages and burials, 1775-7.
See also Edmond Castle

Holm Cultram

GILBANKS, W.F. 'The oldest register book of the parish of Holm Cultram, Cumberland', *C.W.A.A.S., Tr.* **10**, 1889, 176-85. General discussion, including some extracts.

SWIFT, F.B., ed. *The registers of Holm Cultram, 1580-1597. C.W.A.A.S., P.R.S.* **34**. Penrith: the Society, 1948.

Ings

READE, GEO. E.P. 'The Ings registers', *C.W.A.A.S., Tr.* N.S. **13**, 1913, 79-84. Brief note.

Kendal

MOSER, G.E. 'Kendal parish church registers', *C.W.A.A.S., Tr.* **3**, 1878, 49-63. General discussion.

The registers of Kendal, Westmorland. C.W.A.A.S., P.R.S. **7**, **8**, **36** & **39**. 1921-60. Pt.1. 1558-1587, ed. Henry Brierly. Pt.2. Marriages and burials, 1558-1587; baptisms, 1591-1595, ed. Henry Brierly. Pt.3. Baptisms, 1596-9; 1607-31; marriages and burials, 1591-9, ed. R.N. Birley. Pt.4. Marriages and burials, 1606-31, ed. R.N. Birley.

DICKINSON, ROBERT. *Index to Kendal parish registers, 1591-1631. C.W.A.A.S., P.R.S.* 1973.

BATERDEN, JAMES RAE, ed. 'The Catholic registers of Kendal, (Westmorland), 1762-1840, with notes on the mission of Dodding Green from 1706', in *Miscellanea.* Publications of the Catholic Record Society **32**, 1932, 45-116.

Kendal *continued*

NICHOLSON, FRANCIS. 'Kendal (Unitarian) Chapel and its registers', *C.W.A.A.S., Tr.* N.S. **5**, 1905, 172-80. Includes brief note on the register, 1687-1839. See also below, section 12, under Unitarians.

Kentmere

'Kentmere marriages, 1700-1812', *C.F.H.S.N.* **35**, 1985, 17-18. 1702-1812.

Keswick

See Crosthwaite

Kirkandrews on Esk

FERGUSON, R.S. 'The registers and account books of the parish of Kirkandrews-upon-Esk', *C.W.A.A.S., Tr.* **8**, 1886, 280-306. General discussion, with a few extracts.

Kirkby Lonsdale

CONDER, EDWARD. 'The Kirkby Lonsdale parish registers, 1538-1812', *C.W.A.A.S., Tr.* N.S. **5**, 1905, 213-42. Includes many extracts, but not a full transcript.

Kirklinton

'Marriages at Kirklinton', *C.F.H.S.N.* **10**, 1979, 12-13. 1760-66.

Kirkoswald

THORNLEY, JOHN J., ed. *The ancient church registers of the parish of Kirkoswald, Cumberland: Births, marriages, burials, 1577-1812.* Workington: G.H. Smith & Co., 1901. 'Marriages at Kirkoswald', *C.F.H.S.N.* **9**, 1978, 19. 1750-65.

Lamplugh

HASWELL, FRANCIS, ed. *The registers of Lamplugh, 1581-1812. C.W.A.A.S., P.R.S.* **24**, 1936. Includes list of rectors.

Lanercost

WILLIS, T.W., ed. *The register of the parish of Lanercost, Cumberland: baptisms, weddings and burials.* 2 vols. Beverley: Isaac B. Hodgson (v.2 by Wright & Hoggard), 1908-12. v.1. 1666-1730. v.2. 1731-1837.

Lowther

HASWELL, J.F., ed. *The registers of Lowther, 1540-1812. C.W.A.A.S., P.R.S.* **21**, 1933.

Mardale

HASWELL, F. *The register book of Mardale Chappel (Westmorland).* Penrith: George Reel, 1898. 1684-1824.

Martindale

BRIERLY, HENRY, ed. *The registers of Martindale, Westmorland.* Wigan: Strowger & Son, 1907. 1633-1904. Includes biographical notes on incumbents, monumental inscriptions, lists of chapelwardens, overseers, constables, and tenants, etc.

Matterdale

BRIERLY, HENRY, ed. *The registers of Matterdale church, 1634-1720.* Kendal: Titus Wilson, 1908.

Middleton in Lonsdale

HASWELL, J.F., ed. *The registers of Middleton-in-Lonsdale, Westmorland, 1670-1812. C.W.A.A.S., P.R.S.* **12**, 1925. Includes list of vicars, 1718-1894.

Milburn

BRIERLEY, HENRY, ed. *The registers of Milburn, Westmorland, 1679-1812. C.W.A.A.S., P.R.S.* **2**, 1913.

Millom

HASWELL, J.F., ed. *The registers of Millom, Cumberland, 1591-1812. C.W.A.A.S., P.R.S.* **11**, 1925. Includes list of vicars.
See also Waberthwaite

Moresby

ALLEN, H.J., ed. 'Marriages at Moresby, 1676 to [1837]', in PHILLIMORE, W.P.W., & RUSTON-HARRISON, C.W., eds. *C.P.R.M.* **1**, *P.P.R.S.* **130**. Phillimore, 1910, 103-33 & 185-92.

Morland

The registers of Morland. C.W.A.A.S., P.R.S. **38**. Durham: the Society, 1957-. Pt.1. 1538-1742. No more published.

Newbiggin

HASWELL, J.F., ed. *The registers of Newbiggen (Westmorland), 1571-1812. C.W.A.A.S., P.R.S.* **15**, 1927. Includes list of rectors, 1313-1887.

Newton Reigny

HASWELL, J.F., ed. *The registers of Newton Reigny, 1571-1812. C.W.A.A.S., P.R.S.* **22**, 1934. Includes list of incumbents, 1593-1931.

Orton

NICHOLSON, J. HOLME. 'The parish registers of Orton, Westmorland', *C.W.A.A.S., Tr.* **11**, 1891, 250-65. General discussion, including a few extracts, with 'the names of the sworne men', 1596.

Penrith

HASWELL, FRANCIS, ed. *The registers of St.Andrews parish church, Penrith.* 5 vols. *C.W.A.A.S., P.R.S.* **26-30**, 1938-42. Vol.1. 1556-1604. Vol.2. 1605-1660. Vol.3. 1661-1713. Vol.4. 1714-1769. Vol.5. 1770-1812.

WATSON, GEORGE. *Bygone Penrith: a popular arrangement of the Penrith parish registers.* Penrith: J. Atkinson Sweeten, 1893. Pt.1. 1556-1601. No more parts issued.

'Workhouse births', *C.F.H.S.N.* **41**, 1986, 17. Penrith workhouse register of births, 1857.

Ravenstone Dale

METCALFE, R.W. *The Ravenstonedale parish registers.* 3 vols. Kendal: T. Wilson, 1893-4. Covers 1571-1812. Vol.3 includes nonconformist registers.

Saint Bees

STOUT, H.B., ed. *The registers of St.Bees, Cumberland, 1538-1837.* 3 vols. *C.W.A.A.S., P.R.S.* **41**, 1968. Pt.1. Baptisms, 1538-1837. Pt.2. Burials, 1538-1837. Pt.3. Marriages, 1538-1837.

JACKSON, WILLIAM. 'Extracts from the parish register of St.Bees, with comments upon the same', *C.W.A.A.S., Tr.* **1**, 1874, 287-99. General discussion.

Sebergham

KUPER, M.E. 'Sebergham parish registers', *C.W.A.A.S., Tr.* **9**, 1888, 32-96. Includes many extracts, especially concerning the Denton and Nicolson families, with lists of churchwardens, 1743-1814, and clergy, 18th c.

Shap

NOBLE, MARY E., ed. *The registers of the parish of Shap in the County of Westmorland from 1559 to 1830.* Kendal: Titus Wilson, 1912. See also: NOBLE, MISS. 'Shap registers', *C.W.A.A.S., Tr.* N.S. **11**, 1911, 202-8. General discussion, with some names.

Skelton

BRIERLY, HENRY, & RICHARDSON, R. MORRIS, eds. *The registers of the parish church of Skelton, 1580-1812. C.W.A.A.S., P.R.S.* **6**, 1918. Includes list of clergy officiating at marriages, 1754-1812.

Temple Sowerby

SMITH, B. 'Temple Sowerby marriages, 1700-1755', *C.F.H.S.N.* **22**, 1981, 13.

Stanwix

RUSTON-HARRISON, C.W., ed. 'Marriages at Stanwix, 1662 to 1837', in PHILLIMORE, W.P.W. & RUSTON-HARRISON, C.W., eds. *C.P.R.M.* **2**, *P.P.R.S.* **166**. Phillimore, 1912, 1-56.

Thursby

WILSON, JAMES. 'The earliest register of the parish of Thursby', *C.W.A.A.S., Tr.* **14**, 1897, 121-33. Includes list of churchwardens, 1673-1725, and various extracts, including many relating to the Brisco family.

Waberthwaite

KNOWLES, CANON. 'The earlier registers of Waberthwaite and Millom', *C.W.A.A.S., Tr.* **3**, 1878, 314-20. General discussion.

Warcop

ABERCROMBIE, JOHN, ed. *The registers of Warcop, Westmorland, 1597-1744. C.W.A.A.S., P.R.S.* **3**. Kendal: the Society, 1914. Includes lists of clergy, 1310-1901, and churchwardens, 1687-1812, various names of sidesmen, 17-18th c. list of seat-holders (undated), etc.

Watermillock

MACLEAN, HECTOR, ed. *The registers of Watermillock in the county of Cumberland: baptisms, burials and marriages, 1579-1812.* Kendal: Titus Wilson, 1908.

Westward

WILSON, JAMES. 'The early registers of the parish of Westward', *C.W.A.A.S., Tr.* **13**, 1895, 103-17. Includes many extracts, particularly relating to the Barwise, Brisco and Fletcher families, 17-18th c.

Whicham

HASWELL, J.F., ed. *The registers of Whicham, 1569-1812. C.W.A.A.S., P.R.S.* **13**, 1926. Includes list of rectors, 1535-1894.

Whitehaven

STOUT, H.B., ed. *The registers of St.James, Whitehaven. C.W.A.A.S., P.R.S.* **40**, 1964. Pt.1. Baptisms, 1753-1837. No more published.

CUMBRIA FAMILY HISTORY SOCIETY. *St.Nicholas Church, Whitehaven: marriage register, 1694-1837.* [ ]: C.F.H.S., [1987?].

Wigton

SWIFT, F.B., ed. *The registers of Wigton.* 2 vols. *C.W.A.A.S., P.R.S.* **35** & **37**, 1951-5. Pt.1. 1604-1727. Pt.2. Baptisms, 1728-97; marriages, 1728-81; burials, 1728-79.

Workington

CURWEN, S.P., ed. 'Marriages at Workington, 1670 to [1837]', in PHILLIMORE, W.P.W. & RUSTON-HARRISON, C.W., eds. *C.P.R.M.* **1**, *P.P.R.M.* **130**. Phillimore, 1910, 1-102 & 136-84.

8. PROBATE RECORDS

Probate records—wills, inventories, administration bonds, etc.—are invaluable sources of genealogical information. Wills were proved in a variety of courts; Cumberland and Westmorland were in the dioceses of Carlisle and Chester, and in the Province of York. Pre-Reformation wills proved at Carlisle are edited in:
FERGUSON, R.S., ed. *Testamenta Karleolensia: the series of wills from the prae-Reformation registers of the Bishops of Carlisle, 1353-1386.* *C.W.A.A.S., E.S.* **9**, 1893.

A few 'foreign' wills—of soldiers, sailors, Americans, etc.—proved at Carlisle are listed in:
TURNER, A.N.V. 'Foreign wills proved at Carlisle', *Genealogists magazine* **14**, 1962-4, 420-21.

There is no printed index to post-Reformation Carlisle probate records. For wills from the Archdeaconry of Richmond in the Diocese of Chester, see:
RAINE, JAMES, JUN., ed. *Wills and inventories from the registry of the Archdeaconry of Richmond, extending over portions of the counties of York, Westmerland, Cumberland and Lancaster.* Surtees Society **26**, 1853. Selection, 1442-1579, though mainly 16th c. See also:
R[USSELL], M.M. 'Richmond wills', *C.F.H.S.N.* **56**, 1990, 5. List of Archdeaconry of Richmond wills relating to Cumbria.

Wills proved at the Prerogative Court of York—including many from Cumbria—are edited in:
Testamenta Eboracensia: or wills registered at York illustrative of the history, manners, languages, statistics, etc. of the province of York, from the year MCCC downwards. Surtees Society **4, 30, 45, 53, 79** & **106**. 1836-1902. Title varies. Pt.1. 1316-1430. Pt.2. 1429-67 (includes index to Pt.1). Pt.3. 1395-1491 (also includes marriage licences). Pt.4. 1420-1509 (also includes marriage licences etc.). Pt.5. 1509-31. Pt.6. 1516-51.

Abstracts of wills proved in London are printed in:
CLAY, J.W., ed. *North country wills, being abstracts of wills relating to the counties of York, Nottingham, Northumberland, Cumberland and Westmorland at Somerset House and Lambeth Palace.* Surtees Society **116** & **121**. 1908-12. Vol.1. 1383 to 1558. Vol.2. 1558 to 1604.

An index to Cumbrian wills proved in London is provided by:

Probate Records *continued*

CUMBRIA FAMILY HISTORY SOCIETY. *Index and extracts of Cumbrians in wills proved at the P.C.C.* North Shields: Cumbria Family History Society, 1984. Despite its title, this does *not* index wills from the Prerogative Court of Canterbury, although it does list P.C.C. administrations, 1363-1649. Wills proved in a variety of other courts are included.

A miscellaneous collection of wills is contained in:

'Cumberland and Westmorland wills', *Northern genealogist* **1**, 1895, 174-6 & 234-9. See also **2**, 1896, 34-6 & **3**, 1900, 144-5. Wills of Hudson, Musgrave, Middleton, Bellingham, Baynes, Fleming, Adderton, Partis, Langton, Grayburne, Dodgson, Irwen, Bracken, Lowther, Robinson and North families, 17-18th c.

Two works print numerous Quaker wills:

SOMERVELL, JOHN, ed. *Some Westmorland wills, 1686-1738.* Kendal: T. Wilson & Son, 1928. A collection of Quaker wills.

COLLINGWOOD, W.G. 'A book of old Quaker wills', *C.W.A.A.S., Tr.* N.S. **29**, 1929, 1-38. 68 wills, 18th c.

Many individual wills have been published separately, and are listed here by surname:

Allison

'A Wigton man's will', *C.F.H.S.N.* **37**, 1985, 11. Will of John Allison, 1791, with monumental inscription.

Backhouse

FOSTER, JOSEPH, ed. *Wills and administrations of the various Backhouse families registered in the Archdeaconry Court of Richmond, deposited at Somerset House, and at Lancaster, together with others from Somerset House, York and Carlisle.* Chiswick Press, 1894. Westmorland, Cumberland, London, Berkshire and Lancashire; includes pedigrees.

Barwick

'Dean Barwick and his will', *C.W.A.A.S., Tr.* N.S. **65**, 1965, 240-82. 1664. Barwick was Dean of St.Paul's, London. Includes pedigree, 17th c., and various deeds, etc., relating to the Barwick charity at Witherslack, 17-19th c.

Benn

[STEEL, J.P., ed.] *Wills of the family of Benn and others, in that part of Cumberland formerly known as the Copeland Deanery of the Archdeaconry of Richmond, Yorkshire, between the years 1574 and 1677* ... J.P. Steel, 1913.

Benson

COCKERILL, T. 'Bensons of Waberthwaite', *C.F.H.S.N.* **4**, 1977, 12. Three 17-18th c. Benson wills.

Blaykling

HARPER, KENNETH. 'Some interesting documents from Ainstable', *C.W.A.A.S., Tr.* N.S. **50**, 1950, 171-3. Includes will of Thomas Blaykling, 1796.

Blencowe

DUDBRIDGE, JILL. 'Margaret Blencowe', *C.F.H.S.N.* **41**, 1986, 4-5. Will, 1590.

Boulton

BOULTON, C.H. 'Will of Henry Boulton 1748', *C.F.H.S.N.* **22**, 1982, 6-7. Of Kendal, Westmorland.

Bowes

HUDLESTON, C. ROY. 'Elizabeth Bowes of Penrith', *C.W.A.A.S., Tr.* N.S. **65**, 1965, 284-90. Will, 1684; also includes will of Agnes Webster, 1719.

Bowskall

RICHARDSON, L.B. 'A Heversham will', *C.F.H.S.N.* **38**, 1986, 13-14. Will of James Bowskall, 1547.

Brockbank

'Brockbank wills', *C.F.H.S.N.* **32**, 1984, 3-4. 16-17th c. wills of Brockbank family.

Curwen

ESHELBY, H.D. 'Some early Richmond wills', *Northern genealogist* **6**, 1903, 1-2. Will of John Curwen of Workington, 1530.

HUDLESTON, C. ROY. 'An 18th-century squire's possessions', *C.W.A.A.S., Tr.* N.S. **57**, 1957, 127-57. Probate inventory of Henry Curwen, 1778.

Fairfax

'Fairfax wills at Carlisle', *Northern genealogist* **1** 1895, 92-3. 1640-65.

Fairlamb

WATERS, R.E. CHESTER. 'Fairlamb', *Miscellanea genealogica et heraldica* N.S. **1**, 1874, 202. List of wills at Durham relating to the Fairlamb family of Northumberland and Cumberland.

Fleming

COLLINGWOOD, W.G. 'The inventory of Mistress Fleming of Skirwith, 1639', *C.W.A.A.S., Tr.* N.S. **28**, 1928, 33-40.

Fletcher

'The will of Henry Fletcher', *C.F.H.S.N.* **17**, 1980, 5-6. Of Dearham, Cumberland, 1790.

Godwin

H[UDLESTON], C.R. 'A Carlisle notary's will', *C.F.H.S.N.* **39**, 1986, 8-10. Will of Jeremy Godwin, 1578.

Harington

DICKINSON, J.C. 'Three pre-Reformation documents concerning South Cumbria', *C.W.A.A.S., Tr.* N.S. **86**, 1986, 129-32. Includes notes on the wills of William, Lord Harington and Thomas Langton, Bisop of Winchester, 1501.

Hawkrigg

COWPER, H.S. 'A Grasmere farmer's sale schedule in 1710', *C.W.A.A.S., Tr.* **13**, 1895, 253-68. Gives many names of creditors of William Hawkrigg, deceased, from his executrix's accounts, together with the names of those who purchased his goods.

Knipe

HORNYOLD-STRICKLAND, H. 'The will of Edward Knipe, a Tudor vicar of Cliburn and Warcop', *C.W.A.A.S., Tr.* N.S. **44**, 1944, 151-9. 1574.

JONES, G.P. 'The Broad Oak charity', *C.W.A.A.S., Tr.* N.S. **65**, 1965, 298-304. Founded by the will of John Knipe, 1734, which is printed.

Lancaster

Y., H.N.G. 'Lancaster of Westmorland: digests of wills of Edmund Lancaster and Joseph Lancaster', *Genealogist* N.S. **24**, 1908, 216. 1755 and 1805.

Langton

See Harington

Lowrie

'Transcript of the will and inventory of Robert Lowrie of the city of Carlisle proved at Carlisle in 1567 ...', *C.F.H.S.N.* **32**, 1984, 7-9.

Machell

FERGUSON, R.S. 'Wills relating to the Dean and Chapter Library at Carlisle: wills of Rev. Machell, Bishops Smith and Nicolson, and Joseph Nicolson', *C.W.A.A.S., Tr.* **4**, 1880, 1-12. 18th c.

HUDLESTON, C. ROY. 'The will of Anthony Machell', *C.W.A.A.S., Tr.* N.S. **64**, 1964, 387-8. 1719.

Nicolson

See Machell

Ollivant

HUDLESTON, C. ROY. 'Captain Thomas Ollivant', *C.W.A.A.S., Tr.* N.S. **48**, 1948, 130-34. Will, 1747.

Ponsonby

BOYES, DR. 'Family of Ponsonby', *C.F.H.S.N.* **7**, 1978, 12-13. List of wills, 16-18th c.

Postlethwaite

POSTLETHWAITE, S.J. 'Postlethwaite wills and administrations', *C.F.H.S.N.* **58**, 1991, 16-18. List of documents from the Prerogative Court of Canterbury, the Deanery of Copeland, and Carlisle, 18-19th c.

Routledge

HARRISON, J.V. 'Five Bewcastle wills, 1587-1617', *C.W.A.A.S., Tr.* N.S. **67**, 1967, 93-111. Wills of the Routledge family.

Senhouse

HUDLESTON, C. ROY. 'Last will and testament', *C.F.H.S.N.* **37**, 1985, 12-13. Will of William Senhouse, 1671.

Smith

See Machell

Stanley

HUDLESTON, C. ROY. 'Stanley of Cockermouth', *C.W.A.A.S., Tr.* N.S. **72**, 1972, 340-41. Will of Elizabeth Stanley of Embleton, Northumberland, 1713/4.

Walker

JOLLY, M. AIRD. 'The will of John Walker, mariner', *C.W.A.A.S., Tr.* N.S. **45**, 1945, 144-7. Of Kirkoswald, Cumberland, and Kingston on Thames, Surrey, 1805.

Warener

HUDLESTON, C.R. 'The Warener family', *C.W.A.A.S., Tr.* N.S. **68**, 1968, 194. Will of Nicholas Warener, 1583.

Watson

'A will in verse', *C.F.H.S.N.* **37**, 1985, 9. Will of Thomas Watson of Renwick, 1860.

Webster

See Bowes

Wharton

EVANS, JOAN. 'An inventory of Thomas Lord Wharton, 1568', *Archaeological journal* **102**, 1945, 134-50.

'Wills of the Wharton family', *Herald & genealogist* **1**, 1863, 261-4. Wills of Thomas Lord Wharton, 1568, and his widow Anne, 1585, of Healaugh, Yorkshire, and Westmorland.

9. MONUMENTAL INSCRIPTIONS

A. *GENERAL*

Monumental inscriptions are an important source of genealogical information. Many have been published; publications dealing with large parts of the region include:

BOWER, R. 'Brasses in the Diocese of Carlisle', *C.W.A.A.S., Tr.* **13**, 1895, 142-51.

BOWER, CANON. 'Effigies in the Diocese of Carlisle', *C.W.A.A.S., Tr.* **15**, 1899, 417-58.

BOWER, R. 'Busts, portrait medallions, and modern effigies in the churches of the Diocese of Carlisle', *C.W.A.A.S., Tr.* N.S. **4**, 1904, 118-45.

BELLASIS, EDWARD. *Westmorland church notes: being the heraldry, epitaphs, and other inscriptions in the thirty-two ancient parish churches and churchyards of that county.* 2 vols. Kendal: T. Wilson, 1888-9.

SUMMERS, PETER. *Hatchments in Britain, 3: the Northern counties: Cumberland, Westmorland, Durham, Northumberland, Lancashire and Yorkshire.* London: Phillimore, 1980.

Cumbrians buried in Liverpool and Westminster Abbey respectively are listed in:

'Cumbrians in Gibson's Liverpool epitaphs, ref H929/5 Liverpool R.O.', *C.F.H.S.N.* **29**, 1983, 26-7.

HINDS, J.P. 'Local worthies buried in Westminster Abbey', *C.W.A.A.S., Tr.* N.S. **4**, 1904, 104-17.

B. *BY PLACE*

Barton

See Yanwath

Bewcastle

GILCHRIST, GEORGE. *Memorials of Bewcastle.* Annan: the author, 1973. Duplicated typescript; 269 memorials.

Bridekirk

See Brigham

Brigham

WAKE, HENRY THOMAS. *All the monumental inscriptions in the graveyards of Brigham and Bridekirk, near Cockermouth, in the county of Cumberland, from 1666 to 1876.* Cockermouth: Wake, 1878.

Caldbeck

WILSON, JAMES. *Monumental inscriptions in the church and churchyard of Caldbeck, Cumberland.* Dalston: William Beck, 1897. 261 inscriptions.

Carlisle

FERGUSON, R.S. 'The monuments in Carlisle Cathedral', *C.W.A.A.S., Tr.* 7, 1884, 259-70. General discussion, including list of bishops buried in the Cathedral.

FIELD, F.J. 'Heraldry at Carlisle Cathedral', *C.W.A.A.S., Tr.* N.S. **34**, 1934, 22-9.

FERGUSON, MARGARET J., ed. *The monumental inscriptions in the church and churchyard of St.Cuthbert, Carlisle.* Carlisle: Moss, 1889. Includes 555 inscriptions. For corrections and additions, see: HUDLESTON, C. ROY. 'St.Cuthbert's churchyard, Carlisle', *C.W.A.A.S., Tr.* N.S. **63**, 1963, 290-91 & **66**, 1966, 470.

Cleator

POOLEY, JOHN, & POOLEY, BRIAN. *Pre 1800 memorial inscriptions and history of St.Leonards Church, Cleator.* Egremont: C.F.H.S., 1985. Includes list of clergy, 1189-1905 and churchwardens, 1729-1909.

Cockermouth

SMITH, D. 'Monumental inscriptions of All Saints, Cockermouth', in *Cockermouth miscellany.* C.F.H.S., [1987?].

Crosscanonby

SMITH, D., & REED, E. *The memorial inscriptions of the old church yard of the church of St.John the Evangelist, Crosscanonby.* [ ]: Cumbria Family History Society, 1983. Includes 176 inscriptions.

Dalston

WILSON, JAMES. *The monumental inscriptions of the church, churchyard and cemetery of St.Michael's, Dalston, Cumberland.* Dalston: W.R. Beck, 1890. 404 inscriptions.

Edenhall

HASWELL, J.F. 'Heraldic glass in Edenhall church', *C.W.A.A.S., Tr.* **15**, 1899, 111-13.

Grasmere

JACKSON, CHARLES. 'Church notes at Grasmere, Westmorland', *Miscellanea genealogica et heraldica* N.S. **3**, 1880, 145-6 & 153-6. Monumental inscriptions.

Greystoke

LEES, T. 'Greystoke church, descriptive: its vestry or reclusiorum and its monuments', *C.W.A.A.S., Tr.* **1**, 1874, 323-7.

Harrington

'Names of mariners from Harrington lost at sea', *C.F.H.S.N.* **11**, 1979, 15-16. From monumental inscriptions.

Hornby Hall

HASWELL, J.F. 'Notes on local heraldry', *C.W.A.A.S., Tr.* **14**, 1897, 160-64. At Hornby Hall and Penrith church.

Kirkandrews on Esk

GILCHRIST, GEORGE. *Memorials of Kirkandrews on Esk parish (England).* Annan: [George Gilchrist], 1973. 250 memorials. Duplicated typescript.

Kirkby Lonsdale

BOUMPHREY, R.S. 'Heraldry in the window of the Middleton chapel, St.Mary's church, Kirkby Lonsdale', *C.W.A.A.S., Tr.* N.S. **82**, 1982, 201-2.

Kirkoswald

BOUMPHREY, R.S. 'Heraldry at The College, Kirkoswald', *C.W.A.A.S., Tr.* N.S. **77**, 1977, 169-72.

Lanercost Abbey

BROWN, G. BALDWIN, & WHITEHEAD, H. 'The monuments in the choir and transepts of Lanercost Abbey', *C.W.A.A.S., Tr.* **12**, 1893, 312-43. Includes a note on the Dacre family, including a pedigree, 17th c., by J. Wilson.

WHITEHEAD, H. 'The monuments in the nave and aisle of Lanercost Abbey', *Transactions of the Cumberland and Westmorland Association for the Advancement of Literature and Science* 17, 1891-2, 113-23.

Levens Hall

BOUMPHREY, R.S. 'The heraldry at Levens Hall, Westmorland', *C.W.A.A.S., Tr.* N.S. **72**, 1972, 205-15.

Mardale

RYLANDS, J. PAUL. 'Monumental and other inscriptions in the church and churchyard of Mardale in the county of Westmorland', *Genealogist* N.S. **32**, 1896, 222-7.

Maryport

'Maryport's maritime memorials', *C.F.H.S.N.* **21**, 1981, 19-20.

Scotby

'Scotby Quaker M.I's', *C.F.H.S.N.* **36**, 1985, 5-6.

Stapleton

GILCHRIST, GEORGE. *Memorials of Stapleton.* Annan: the author, 1974. 322 memorials. Duplicated typescript.

Threlkeld

DIXON, C.J. 'Monument in Threlkeld churchyard', *C.F.H.S.N.* **9**, 1978, 11-12. To many followers of the chase.

Whitehaven

COWLEY, D.I. '[Whitehaven monumental inscriptions to men lost at sea or who died abroad]', *C.F.H.S.N.* **9**, 1978, 15-17.

STOUT, H.B., ed. *The monumental inscriptions of the church and churchyard of St James, Whitehaven, Cumberland. C.W.A.A.S., T.S.* **16**, 1963. Includes 282 entries.

Wigton

WILSON, JAMES. *The monumental inscriptions of the parish church and churchyard and the Congregational burial ground, Wigton, Cumberland.* Wigton: T. McMechan, 1892. 568 memorials.

Yanwath

HASWELL, FRANCIS. 'On armorial stones at Yanwath and Barton church', *C.W.A.A.S., Tr.* N.S. **4**, 1904, 85-8. Includes pedigree of the Bowman family of Askham, Westmorland, 16-19th c.

C. *BY FAMILY*

Aglionby

WRIGHT, G.W. 'Rubrication in churchyard inscriptions', *Notes & queries* **153**, 1927, 6-7. See also 68. Inscription to Henry Aglionby, 1853.

Clifford

FERGUSON, R.S. 'The tombs of (i) Margaret, Countess Dowager of Cumberland, and (ii) Anne, Countess Dowager of Pembroke, Dorset and Montgomery, in Appleby church', *C.W.A.A.S., Tr.* **8**, 1886, 174-85. Clifford family, 1616 and 1675.

Dacre

BOUCH, J. LOWTHER. 'A note on the tombstone of Ranulph, Lord de Dacre of Gillesland in Saxton churchyard, Yorkshire', *C.W.A.A.S., Tr.* N.S. **16**, 1916, 229-31. 1461.

Denton

See Relph

Fleming

BOUMPHREY, R.S. 'Heraldry at Rydal Hall', *C.W.A.A.S., Tr.* N.S. **75**, 1975, 132-5. Fleming family.

Hudleston

COWPER, H. SWAINSON. 'Notes on the Hudleston monuments and heraldry at Millom', *C.W.A.A.S., Tr.* **12**, 1893, 129-32.

Hutton

HASWELL, FRANCIS. 'The Hutton effigies in St.Andrews church, Penrith', *C.W.A.A.S., Tr.* N.S. **43**, 1943, 147-60. Includes pedigrees, 17th c., and will of Elizabeth Hutton, 1671.

WATSON, GEORGE. 'The Hutton effigies now in Great Salkeld churchyard, formerly in Penrith church', *C.W.A.A.S., Tr.* **13**, 1895, 420-30. Includes pedigree, 15-18th c.

Musgrave

WATSON, GEORGE. 'Two lintel inscriptions: the Musgraves of Edenhall and some of their descendants', *C.W.A.A.S., Tr.* **15**, 1899, 82-104. Includes extracts from Penrith parish register, 16-18th c.

Pickering

HASWELL, FRANCIS. 'The Pickering shield of arms at Crosby Ravensworth Hall', *C.W.A.A.S., Tr.* N.S. **8**, 1908, 82-3. 14-16th c.

Relph

FERGUSON, R.S. 'The Relph and Denton monuments in Sebergham church', *C.W.A.A.S., Tr.* **7**, 1884, 253-8. Includes will of Joseph Relph, 1742/3.

Tyrer

WILSON, EDWARD M. 'Ralph Tyrer, B.D., Vicar of Kendal 1592-1627', *C.W.A.A.S., Tr.* N.S. **78**, 1978, 71-84. Monumental inscriptions, 1627.

Wilson

HUDLESTON, C. ROY. 'A Westmorland customs officer', *C.W.A.A.S., Tr.* N.S. **68**, 1968, 192-4. Inscription to Anthony Wilson, 1718.

Wood

BROWN, R. PERCIVAL. 'Christopher Wood's inscription in Kirkby Lonsdale church', *C.W.A.A.S., Tr.* N.S. **25**, 1925, 321-30. 16-17th c.

Wordsworth

JACKSON, WM. 'Wordsworthiana: Grasmere churchyard', *Miscellanea genealogica et heraldica* N.S. **3**, 1880, 188. 19th c.

10. OFFICIAL LISTS OF NAMES

Government bureaucracy frequently requires the compilation of lists of names; these served a wide range of purposes. For England as a whole, the earliest such list was Domesday Book. This record is fragmentary for Cumbria; the return, such as it is, is printed in the *Victoria County History* volume (see above, section 1).

Taxation Lists
From the medieval period until the seventeenth century, the subsidy provided one of the main sources of government revenue. This role was taken over by the hearth tax after the Restoration. The records of these two taxes are an important source for genealogists. For a general discussions of the subsidy, see:

BECKETT, J.V. 'Westmorland's book of rates', *C.W.A.A.S., Tr.* N.S. **76**, 1976, 127-37. General discussion of the basis of assessments to the subsidy.

FRASER, C.M. 'The Cumberland and Westmorland lay subsidies for 1332', *C.W.A.A.S., Tr.* N.S. **66**, 1966, 131-58.

A transcript of the subsidy roll for 1335/6 is printed in:

STEEL, J.P. *Cumberland lay subsidy: being the account of a fifteenth and tenth collected 6th Edward III*. Kendal: Titus Wilson, 1912.

A general discussion of the hearth tax and other new taxes is provided by:

BECKETT, J.V. 'Local custom and the new taxation in the seventeenth and eighteenth centuries: the example of Cumberland', *Northern history* **12**, 1976, 105-26.

A number of transcripts for particular places have been printed.

Barton
'Chimney money', *C.F.H.S.N.* **33**, 1984, 3-6. Includes transcript of hearth tax for Barton, 1669-72.

Brampton
'A Cumberland hearth tax', *C.F.H.S.N.* **4**, 1977, 2-3. For Brampton, c.1664.

Kendal Barony
CONDER, EDWARD. 'The hearth tax return, 22nd Charles II, Kendal Barony', *C.W.A.A.S., Tr.* N.S. **19**, 1919, 140-50.

Ravenstone Dale
'Hearth tax roll for Ravenstonedale, 1669-72', *C.F.H.S.N.* **5**, 1977, 13.

Uldale
HUGHES, M.H. 'Householders in Uldale in 1662', *C.F.H.S.N.* **26**, 1983, 8-9. Hearth tax return.

The poll-tax returns for Carlisle in 1377 are also available:

KIRBY, J.L. 'The poll-tax of 1377 for Carlisle', *C.W.A.A.S., Tr.* N.S. **58**, 1958, 110-17.

Loyalty Oaths
Governments demand loyalty from their subjects. Sometimes they also demand an oath of loyalty. At the outbreak of the Great Rebellion, Parliament demanded an oath of loyalty from everyone over eighteen. The signatures of those who took the 'protestation' oath now constitute a major source of information on the inhabitants of seventeenth-century England, providing an almost complete 'census' of the adult male population. The returns for Westmorland are printed in:

FARADAY, M.A., ed. *The Westmorland protestation returns, 1641/2. C.W.A.A.S., T.S.* **17**, 1971.

The return for a single Cumberland parish is printed in:

CLAY, CHARLES. 'Caldbeck in 1642', *C.W.A.A.S., Tr.* N.S. **21**, 1921, 276-9.

Poll Books, etc.
In the eighteenth and early nineteenth centuries, the names of Parliamentary electors were frequently recorded in poll books and lists of freeholders, etc., which were sometimes published. Full details of these are provided in the works listed in *English genealogy: an introductory bibliography*, section 12D. They are also listed in Hodgson's *Bibliography* (above, section 2). A brief list of freeholders in Lonsdale Ward is given in:

'Westmorland ... A list of the freeholders ... within Lonsdale Ward ... 1729', *C.F.H.S.N.* **21**, 1981, 13.

For the pollbook of Cockermouth, 1737, see Steel's paper, listed below, section 13A.

The Census
By far the most useful lists are those deriving from the official census. Nationally, these began in 1801; however, in 1787 the Westmorland Quarter Sessions directed that a full census be taken of the county. The surviving returns, giving names of all the inhabitants in the parishes covered, have been printed in:

ASHCROFT, LORAINE. *Vital statistics: the Westmorland census of 1787*. Curwen Archives text, **1**. Kendal: Curwen Archives Trust, 1992.

The Census *continued*

The Cumbria Family History Society has published many transcripts and indexes of the 1851 return:

CUMBRIA FAMILY HISTORY SOCIETY. *Transcript of the 1851 census of Allhallows, Bolton: HO107/2433, folios 262-305.* [ ]: C.F.H.S., [1988].

CUMBRIA FAMILY HISTORY SOCIETY. *Transcript and index of the 1851 census of Cockermouth (HO107/2434; folios 330-415).* [ ]: C.F.H.S., [1989].

CUMBRIA FAMILY HISTORY SOCIETY. *Transcript and index of the 1851 census of Corney, Bootle, Whitbeck, Whicham, Chapel Sucken, Millom Below, Upper Millom, Thwaites and Ulpha.* [ ]: C.F.H.S., [1991].

CUMBRIA FAMILY HISTORY SOCIETY. *Transcript of the 1851 census of Grasmere, Langdale, Rydal, & Loughrigg: HO107/2441, folios 1-50.* [ ]: C.F.H.S., [1986].

CUMBRIA FAMILY HISTORY SOCIETY. *Transcript of the 1851 census of Hugill & Kentmere, Over Staveley, Nether Staveley.* [ ]: C.F.H.S., [1986].

CUMBRIA FAMILY HISTORY SOCIETY. *Transcript & index for the 1851 census for Kendal (part 1) (HO107/2442, folios 5-110).* [ ]: C.F.H.S., 1989.

CUMBRIA FAMILY HISTORY SOCIETY. *Transcript of the 1851 census of Killington, Middleton, Barbon & Casterton: HO107/2441, folios 431-479.* [ ]: C.F.H.S., [1988?].

SMITH, D. *An index to the 1851 census of Leath Ward of Cumberland.* 2 vols. Dearham: C.F.H.S., 1983-7. Pt.1. Penrith Town. Pt.2. Penrith District.

CUMBRIA FAMILY HISTORY SOCIETY. *Transcript of the 1851 census of Undermilbeck North, Undermilbeck South, Crook: HO107/2441, folios 139-164.* [ ]: C.F.H.S., [1986].

CUMBRIA FAMILY HISTORY SOCIETY. *Transcript and index for the 1851 census for Wasdale, Eskdale, Iton, Drigg, Muncaster, Waberthwaite (HO107/2438, folios 1-90).* [ ]: C.F.H.S., [1989].

CUMBRIA FAMILY HISTORY SOCIETY. *Transcript and index for the 1851 census for Wetheral, Warwick, Scotby, Crosby, Walby: (HO107/2429, folios 5-148).* [ ]: C.F.H.S., 1990.

CUMBRIA FAMILY HISTORY SOCIETY. *Transcript of the 1851 census of Woodside: HO107/2433, folios 310-351.* [ ]: C.F.H.S., [1988].

Cumbrians in other places in 1851 are listed in:

'Cumbrians in 1851 census for Alnwick', *C.F.H.S.N.* 53, 1989, 6-8. Alnwick is in Northumberland.

PARK, P.B. *An index to Cumbrians in Liverpool, 1851.* [Walton on Thames]: C.F.H.S., [1986]. Pt.1. Liverpool Sub-districts 1-4. Pt.2. Liverpool Sub-districts 5-7. To be completed. Corrections to this work are printed in: 'Cumbrians in Liverpool', *C.F.H.S.N.* 61, 1991, 11-12.

The only other census material in print is: 'The iron miners of Eskdale, 1881', *C.F.H.S.N.* 27, 1983, 10-12. Lists miners in census, giving ages and places of birth. Many were Cornish. A major project is currently under way to index the whole of the 1881 census. When this is complete, it will be published on microfiche.

Landowners Census

A census of a different kind was conducted in 1873. It listed everyone who owned more than one acre of land. The returns are published in:

Return of owners of land, 1873: Westmorland. House of Commons Parliamentary papers, 1874, 72, pt.2, 485-502.

Return of owners of land, 1873: Cumberland. House of Commons Parliamentary papers, 1874, 72, pt.1, 193-230.

11. DIRECTORIES AND MAPS, ETC.

Directories are an invaluable source for identifying people in the past. For the nineteenth century, they are the equivalent of the modern phone book. Many directories for Cumberland and Westmorland were published; unfortunately, they tend to be scarce (except for those which have been reprinted). I have listed all those I have actually seen, plus a few for which citations have been given in two or more reference works. The emphasis is on the nineteenth century. Other directories may be identified in Hodgson's *Bibliography* and in the works cited in *English genealogy: an introductory bibliography*, section 13. The following list is arranged chronologically:

JOLLIE, FRANCIS. *Jollie's Cumberland guide and directory, containing a descriptive tour through the county and a list of persons in public and private situations in every principal place in the county* ... Carlisle: Jollie & Sons, 1811. Includes biographical notes on eminent Cumbrians.

PARSON, WILLIAM, & WHITE, WILLIAM. *A history, directory and gazetteer of Cumberland and Westmorland, with that part of the Lake District in Lancashire, forming the lordships of Furness and Cartmel.* Beckermet: Michael Moon, 1976. Originally published Leeds: W. White & Co., 1829.

National commercial directory ... of Chester, Cumberland, Durham, Lancaster, Northumberland, Westmoreland and York ... Pigot, 1834.

MANNIX & WHELLAN. *History, gazetteer and directory of Cumberland.* Beckermet: Michael Moon, 1974. Originally published Beverley: W.B. Johnson, 1847. This is indexed in: GRIGG, R. *The principal inhabitants of Cumberland in 1847: an alphabetical index.* Warrington: Beewood Coldell, 1990.

MANNEX, P.J. *History, topography and directory of Westmorland and Lonsdale North of the Sands, in Lancashire, together with a descriptive and geological view of the whole of the Lake District.* Simpkin Marshall & Co., 1849.

MANNEX & CO. *A history, topography and directory of Westmorland, and of the Hundreds of Lonsdale and Amounderness in Lancashire.* Beckermet: Michael Moon, 1978. Originally published Beverley: W.B. Johnson, 1851.

Slater's royal national commercial directory of the northern counties. Vol.2: Cheshire, Cumberland, Lancashire and Westmorland. Manchester: I. Slater, 1855.

Post Office directory of Westmoreland, Cumberland, Northumberland and Durham. Kelly & Co., 1858-1938. 15 issues. Title varies; sometimes *Kelly's directory* ... The portions for each county were also issued separately, or with different combinations of counties, on occasion.

MORRIS, HARRISON & CO. *Commercial directory and gazetteer of the county of Cumberland.* Nottingham: Morris, Harrison & Co., 1861.

Mercer and Crocker's general topographical and historical directory and gazetteer for the principal towns and villages in Cumberland, Westmorland, North Riding of York, the County of Durham and Newcastle, Sunderland ... Newcastle on Tyne: Mercer & Crocker, 1869.

Slater's royal national commercial directory of Cheshire, Cumberland and Westmorland ... Manchester: Slater, 1869.

Slater's royal national commercial directory of the counties of Cumberland, Durham, Northumberland, Westmorland, with the Cleveland district ... I. Slater, 1876-84. 4 issues.

Postal directory for 1882 of Cumberland. F. Porter, 1882.

History topography and directory of West Cumberland. Preston: T. Bulmer, 1883.

History topography and directory of East Cumberland. Manchester: T. Bulmer & Co., 1884.

T. BULMER & CO. *History, topography and directory of Westmoreland, comprising its history and archaeology, a general view of its physical and geographical features, with separate historical and topographical descriptions of each town, parish, and manor; also a list of residences of the nobility and gentry.* Preston: T. Bulmer & Co., 1885-1906. 2 issues.

T. BULMER & CO. *History, topography and directory of Cumberland, comprising its history and archaeology: a general view of its physical and geological features with separate historical and topographical descriptions of each town, parish, manor, and extra-parochial liberty.* Penrith: T.F. Bulmer, 1901. This directory includes much historical information amounting to a full parochial survey.

Cumberland and Westmorland directory. Walsall: Aubrey & Co., 1937-9. 3 issues.

Carlisle

The Carlisle directory and guide, containing an historical account of the ancient and present state of that celebrated city, with alphabetical lists of the gentry, clergy, bankers, professors of physic, law, manufacturers and traders ... Carlisle:

Carlisle *continued*

Launcelot Smith, [1792]. Offprinted from the *Universal British directory.*

A picture of Carlisle and directory ... Carlisle: A. Henderson, 1810. Includes 'list of the principal merchants, tradesmen and others'.

The Carlisle directory ... for ... 1837. Carlisle: James Steel, 1837.

A directory and local guide or hand book to Carlisle and immediate vicinity. Carlisle: H. Scott, 1858.

Directory of the city of Carlisle. Carlisle: C. Thurnam, 1870.

P.J. Jackson & Co's postal address directory of the city of Carlisle ... including the principal towns and adjacent villages of Cumberland and Westmorland ... Newcastle on Tyne: P.J. Jackson & Co., 1880.

Arthur's directory of Carlisle, with a map of the suburbs and a directory of Stanwix, Edentown, Etterby, Rickerby, Stainton, Botcherby & Harraby. Carlisle: A. Barnes Moss, 1880.

A.B. Moss' post office directory of Carlisle, and directory of Stanwix, Edentown, Etterby, Stainton, Botcherby and Harraby. Carlisle: A. Barnes-Moss, 1884.

Clarkes business directory of Carlisle and Wigton. Glasgow: C. Clarke, 1893.

Middleton's commercial directory of Carlisle, 1893-4. Workington: A.E. Middleton, 1894.

Post Office Carlisle directory, including Botcherby, Edentown, Etterby, Harraby, Stanwix and Stainton. Carlisle: Beaty, 1902-13. 5 issues.

Carlisle directory, including suburbs. Carlisle: Garty & Hudson, 1907-20. Later editions published by Carlisle and District Chamber of Trade.

CARLISLE AND DISTRICT CHAMBER OF TRADE. *Carlisle directory.* Carlisle: Beaty, 1920-40. 7 issues.

Windermere

MARTINEAU, HARRIET. *Guide to Windermere with tours to the neighbouring lakes and other interesting places.* Windermere: John Garnett, 1854-1856. 3 editions. The fourth (c.1858) has no directory.

Workington

Clarkes business directory of Workington, Harrington, Maryport & Whitehaven. Glasgow: C. Clarke, 1893.

Workington *continued*

Middleton's commercial directory for Workington. Workington: A.E. Middleton & Co., 1904.

Maps

Directories sometimes, usefully, include maps, which you will need to consult in order to locate particular places. All genealogists should consult the sheet maps showing parish boundaries published by the Institute of Heraldic and Genealogical Studies. Early maps reveal a great deal about the way in which the landscape has changed. A useful edition of an early Ordnance Survey map is provided by:

The Old Series Ordnance Survey maps of England and Wales ... volume VIII: Northern England and the Isle of Man. Lympne Castle: Harry Margary, 1991.

Individual sheet maps of the 1st edition O.S. maps have been reprinted by the publisher David & Charles.

Many early printed maps are listed in:

CURWEN, JOHN F. 'The chorography, or, a descriptive catalogue of the printed maps of Cumberland and Westmorland', *C.W.A.A.S., Tr.* N.S. **18**, 1918, 1-92.

Reference must also be made to the sheet parish maps published by the Institute of Heraldic and Genealogical Studies, which should be in the possession of every genealogist. Even the best maps do not necessarily show every place-name that one comes across in genealogical research. If you need to locate an obscure place-name, and cannot find it on the map, consult one of the volumes published by the English Place Name Society:

ARMSTRONG, A.M., MAWER, A., STENTON, F.M., & DICKINS, BRUCE. *The place-names of Cumberland.* 3 vols. English Place Name Society **20-22**, 1950-52.

SMITH, A.H. *The place-names of Westmorland.* 2 vols. English Place Name Society **42-3**, 1967. See also:

SEDGEFIELD, W.J. *The place-names of Cumberland and Westmorland.* English series 7. Manchester: Manchester University Press, 1915. Also published as *C.W.A.A.S., E.S.* **14**.

Dialect

Unfamiliar words in documentary sources may also give problems. There are a number of glossaries of Cumbrian dialect which may prove useful:

A glossary of provincial words used in the county of Cumberland. John Gray Bell, 1851.

DICKINSON, W. *A glossary of the words and phrases pertaining to the dialect of Cumberland*. [Re-arranged ed.] Bemrose & Sons, 1899.

KIRKBY, BRYHAN. *Lakeland words: a collection of dialect words and phrases as used in Cumberland and Westmorland, with illustrative sentences in the North Westmorland dialect*. Kendal: T. Wilson, 1898.

12. RELIGIOUS RECORDS

The importance of the institutional church was formerly much greater than it is today. Consequently, many of the sources essential to the genealogist are to be found in ecclesiastical rather than secular archives—for example, parish registers, wills, local government records. Ecclesiastical sources are to be found throughout this bibliography; this section concentrates on those topics which are primarily to do with the administration of the church. For a general history of the Diocese of Carlisle, see:

FERGUSON, R.S. *Carlisle*. Diocesan histories. S.P.C.K., 1889. Includes lists of bishops, priors and deans. See also Bouch's *Prelates and people*, listed above, section 1.

For brief descriptions of churches in the two counties see:

COX, J. CHARLES. *Cumberland and Westmorland*. County church series. George Allen & Co., 1913.

The Diocese of Carlisle constituted the major portion of the two counties. The registers of its bishops recorded the general business of the diocese. The lists of ordinations and institutions they contain, together with the occasional will, are of particular value to genealogists. One register has been published:

THOMPSON, W.N., ed. *The register of John de Halton, Bishop of Carlisle, A.D. 1292-1324*. 2 vols. Canterbury and York Society **12-13**, 1913. Also published as *C.W.A.A.S., R.S.* **2**.

See also:

RAINE, JAMES, ed. *Historical papers and letters from the northern registers*. Rolls series **61**. H.M.S.O. **1873**. Includes many extracts from ecclesiastical records relating to the Diocese of Carlisle, etc.

SWANSON, R.N. 'Sede vacante administration in the medieval diocese of Carlisle: the accounts of the vacancy of December 1395 to March 1396', *C.W.A.A.S., Tr.* N.S. **90**, 1990, 183-94. Includes register of the Archbishop of York.

The southern part of the region fell within the Archdeaconry of Richmond, in the Diocese of Chester. Its registers are calendared in:

THOMPSON, A. HAMILTON. 'The registers of the Archdeaconry of Richmond', *Yorkshire Archaeological Journal* **25**(98), 129-268.

The Archdeaconry included Westmorland and Copeland in southern Cumberland.

For lists of the senior clergy of the Diocese of Carlisle, see:

Religious Records *continued*

LE NEVE, JOHN. *Fasti ecclesiae Anglicanae, 1066-1300, II: monastic cathedrals (northern and southern provinces)*. Athlone Press, 1971.

LE NEVE, JOHN. *Fasti ecclesiae Anglicanae, 1300-1541, VI: Northern Province (York, Carlisle and Durham)*. comp. B. Jones. Athlone Press, 1963. Lists bishops, priors and archdeacons.

See also:

PRESCOTT, CHANCELLOR. 'The officers of the Diocese of Carlisle', *C.W.A.A.S., Tr.* N.S. **11**, 1911, 90-117. List of Archdeacons, Vicars General, Chancellors and Officials Principal, with biographical notes.

An early poll tax return gives names of many clergy:

KIRBY, J.L. 'Two tax accounts of the Diocese of Carlisle, 1379-80', *C.W.A.A.S., Tr.* N.S. **52**, 1952, 70-84. Poll tax on clergy.

The names of monks granted pensions on the dissolution of the monasteries are given in:

WILSON, JAMES. 'The victims of the Tudor disestablishment in Cumberland and Westmorland during the reign of Edward VI and Mary', *C.W.A.A.S., Tr.* **13**, 1895, 364-88.

Lay leaders names, 16-18th c., are noted in:

BARROW IN FURNESS, BISHOP OF. 'On the readers in the chapelries of the Lake District', *C.W.A.A.S., Tr.* N.S. **5**, 1905, 89-105.

For clergy ejected during the Commonwealth, see:

WILSON, NORMAN F. 'Ejected ministers in Westmorland and Cumberland: minutes of the proceedings of the Committee', *C.W.A.A.S., Tr.* N.S. **24**, 1924, 66-77. 1655-6; includes many names.

Nineteenth and early twentieth century clergy may be identified in:

The Carlisle Diocesan calendar & clergy list ... Carlisle: C. Thurnam & Sons, 1868-1954. Annual.

A number of works describe the diocesan muniments at Carlisle:

BOUCH, C.M. LOWTHER. 'The muniments of the Diocese of Carlisle', *C.W.A.A.S., Tr.* N.S. **46**, 1946, 174-90.

'The Carlisle Cathedral mss', *Second report of the Royal Commission on Historical Manuscripts.* C.441. H.M.S.O., 1874, 123-5.

SHEPPARD, J. BRIGSTOCKE. 'The historical mss. of the see of Carlisle', *Ninth report of the Royal Commission on Historical Manuscripts.* C.3773. H.M.S.O., 1883, 177-96. Includes list of testators whose wills are copied in the 14th c. bishops' registers.

DAVEY, C.R. 'Early diocesan accounts at Carlisle', *Journal of the Society of Archivists* **3**, 1968, 424-5.

Many documents are printed in:

NICOLSON, WILLIAM. *Miscellany accounts of the Diocese of Carlisle, with the terriers delivered in to me at my primary visitation.* ed. R.S. Ferguson. *C.W.A.A.S., E.S.* **1**, 1877. Includes some monumental inscriptions, lists of preachers, etc.

Many histories of particular churches and parishes have been published. These cannot be listed here; consult Hodgson's *Bibliography ...* (see section 2 above). Lists of clergy in particular churches, with other miscellaneous information, are provided by:

Gosforth Deanery

LOFTIE, A.G. *The Rural Deanery of Gosforth, Diocese of Carlisle: its churches and endowments.* Kendal: T. Wilson, 1889. Includes lists of incumbents.

Whitehaven Deanery

CAINE, CEASAR. *A history of the churches of the rural deanery of Whitehaven.* Whitehaven: Halton, 1916. Includes extensive extracts from parish registers.

Aikton

LUCKELY, H.O. 'Rectors of Aikton', *C.W.A.A.S., Tr.* N.S. **37**, 1937, 218-9. List, 1304-1928.

Carlisle. Cathedral

TODD, HUGH. *Notitia ecclesiae Cathedralis Carliolensis et notitia prioratus de Wedderhall.* ed. R.S. Ferguson. *C.W.A.A.S., T.S.* **6**, 1891. Includes lists of priors, deans, etc., at Carlisle and Wetheral.

Carlisle. St.Cuthbert

FERGUSON, R.S. 'The lectureship and lecturers at S.Cuthbert's Church, Carlisle', *C.W.A.A.S., Tr.* **7**, 1884, 312-29. Lists lecturers and other clergy, 17-19th c.

Crosthwaite

EELES, FRANCIS C. *The parish church of St.Kentigern, Crosthwaite.* Carlisle: Charles Thurnam & Sons, 1953. Includes list of ministers, and monumental inscriptions.

Dalston

WILSON, JAMES. 'A list of the rectors and vicars of Dalston', *C.W.A.A.S., Tr.* N.S. **22**, 1922, 1-23. With biographical notes.

Heversham

CURWEN, JOHN F. 'Heversham church', *C.W.A.A.S., Tr.* N.S. **25**, 1925, 28-80. Includes list of rectors and vicars, 13-20th c., with biographical notes, and wills of Roger More of London, 1499, Edward Brown of Lincoln, 1506, Myles Briggis, 1517, Giles Aylephe, 1588 and Jasper Buskell, 1621.

Kendal

BREAY, J. 'Kendal parish church: an history of its organ and organists', *C.W.A.A.S., Tr.* N.S. **45**, 1945, 99-115. Includes list of organists, 1708-1940.

CURWEN, J.F. 'The parish church of Kendal', *C.W.A.A.S., Tr.* **15**, 1900, 157-220. Includes list of clergy, with biographical notes.

Kirkby Lonsdale

BROWN, R. PERCIVAL. 'The vicars of Kirkby Lonsdale', *C.W.A.A.S., Tr.* N.S. **29**, 1929, 166-92. 1245-1917. Includes biographical notices.

WARE, CANON. 'Notes upon the parish church of Kirkby Lonsdale', *C.W.A.A.S., Tr.* **1**, 1874, 189-203. Includes notes on vicars.

'Bible distribution', *C.F.H.S.N.* **57**, 1990, 15. List from Kirkby Lonsdale vestry book of those who received free bibles in 1839. Gives ages and masters.

Kirkoswald

HUGHES, THOMAS CANN. 'Notes on the vicars of Kirkoswald since the Commonwealth', *C.W.A.A.S., Tr.* N.S. **13**, 1913, 287-96.

Mardale

WHITESIDE, J. 'Mardale chapel and the Holmes of Mardale', *C.W.A.A.S., Tr.* N.S. **2**, 1902, 141-50. Includes list of clergy, 1703-1894, and will of John Holme, 1735.

Orton

WHITESIDE, J. 'Orton, Westmorland: the church and some documents in the chest', *C.W.A.A.S., Tr.* N.S. **4**, 1904, 154-82. Includes list of vicars from 1595, with biographical notes.

Stanwix

WOOD, J.R. 'The parish of Stanwix', *C.W.A.A.S., Tr.* **11**, 1891, 286-9. Primarily a list of references to incumbents, 13-18th c.

Swindale

WHITESIDE, J. 'Swindale Chapel', *C.W.A.A.S., Tr.* N.S. **1**, 1901, 256-67. Includes list of clergy, 1730-1901.

Wetheral

See Carlisle. Cathedral

Whitehaven

HOPKINSON, ROBERT. 'The appointment of the first minister of St.Nicholas church, Whitehaven', *C.W.A.A.S., Tr.* N.S. **72**, 1972, 283-302. Includes lists of inhabitants, 1687 and 1693.

Windermere

BRYDSON, A.P. 'Some pre-Reformation clergy of Windermere', *C.W.A.A.S., Tr.* N.S. **20**, 1920, 117-26.

BROWNE, GEORGE. 'The advowson and some of the rectors of Windermere since the Reformation', *C.W.A.A.S., Tr.* N.S. **9**, 1909, 41-77.

Whicham

SYKES, W. SLATER. 'Notes during the restoration of Whicham church', *C.W.A.A.S., Tr.* N.S. **2**, 1902, 322-8. Includes list of rectors, 1278-1894.

Workington

IREDALE, THOMAS. 'The rectors of Workington', *C.W.A.A.S., Tr.* N.S. **10**, 1910, 135-47. List with biographical notes, 1150-1905.

Nonconformists

Many denominations have been active in Cumbria. For a general history of Cumbrian nonconformity, see:

SELL, ALAN P.F. *Church planting: a study of Westmorland nonconformity.* Worthing: Walter, 1986. Many names.

Nonconformist ministers ejected from the Church of England in 1662 are listed in:

NIGHTINGALE, B. *The ejected of 1662 in Cumberland and Westmorland, their predecessors and successors.* 2 vols. Manchester: Manchester U.P., 1911. Arranged by parish; with many biographical notices. An appendix lists the commencement date of parish registers, and an extensive bibliography is included.

The following list of nonconformist histories is not comprehensive, but is intended to indicate works likely to be of interest to genealogists.

Congregationalists

LEWIS, W. *History of the Congregational Church, Cockermouth, being selections from its own records.* Cockermouth: H.K. Judd, 1870. Includes list of church members, 1651-1700, from the baptismal register.

Methodists

BURGESS, JOHN. *A history of Cumbrian Methodism*. Kendal: Titus Wilson & Sons, 1980. Includes a useful list of sources.

WILKINSON, SALLY. 'Ambleside Wesleyan Methodists', *C.F.H.S.N.* **37**, 1985, 8. List of box holders, c.1900.

Presbyterians

PENFOLD, HENRY. 'Early Brampton Presbyterianism, 1662-1780', *C.W.A.A.S., Tr.* N.S. **3**, 1903, 94-123. Many names, including a list of ministers, 17-19th c., and a list of ministers ejected from Cumberland and Westmorland livings in 1662.

WHITEHEAD, H. 'Brampton XVIIth century Presbyterians', *C.W.A.A.S., Tr.* **8**, 1886, 348-72. Includes list of members, 1712.

COLLIGAN, J.H. 'Great Salkeld Presbyterian meeting house', *C.W.A.A.S., Tr.* N.S. **8**, 1908, 41-54. Includes biographical notices of ministers, 18-19th c., notes on the families of Benson, Rotheram, and Threlkeld; and notes on 19th c. deeds.

SCOTT, DANIEL. *Some old Penrith records: the story of the Presbyterian church as told in the registers*. Penrith: R. Scott, [1899]. Reprinted from *Penrith Observer*. Brief notes on the registers of births, marriages and deaths.

COLLIGAN, JAMES H. 'Penruddock Presbyterian meeting house', *C.W.A.A.S., Tr.* N.S. **5**, 1905, 150-71. Includes a list of meeting house deeds, and notes on ministers.

Quakers

FERGUSON, RICHARD S. *Early Cumberland and Westmorland Friends: a series of biographical sketches of early members of the Society in those counties*. F. Bowyer Kitts, 1871.

'Cumbrians in Hartshaw monthly meeting records', *C.F.H.S.N.* **40**, 1986, 9-10. Presumably Lancashire Quakers, 1798-1832, who married Cumbrian brides.

Quakers *continued*

SOUTHEY, ROSEMARY. 'Quaker records', *C.F.H.S.N.* **50**, 1989, 15-17. List of Quakers from Cumbria in Newcastle upon Tyne, 19th c.

MONCRIEFF, MRS. 'A Quaker marriage in 1852', *C.F.H.S.N.* **25**, 1982, 3-4. Includes a list of numerous witnesses at the marriage of Isaac Fearon and Ann Robinson, 1852 at Pardshaw.

Roman Catholics

DONAL, GILBERT. *A short history of Catholicism in West Cumberland*. Whitehaven: [ ], 1932. Reprinted from *Whitehaven Catholic Magazine*. Includes useful notes on particular churches.

HILTON, J.A. 'The Cumbrian Catholics', *Northern history* **16**, 1980, 40-58.

VAUGHAN, F.J. 'The Border Catholics in 1687', *C.F.H.S.N.* **27**, 1983, 5-6. List of 126 confirmed at Corby Castle.

HUDLESTON, C. ROY. 'Cumberland recusants of 1723/4', *C.W.A.A.S., Tr.* N.S. **59**, 1959, 115-38. Biographical notices of 11 recusants, with some probate records.

WORRALL, E.S. *Return of papists, 1767: Diocese of Chester*. Occasional publication **1**, Catholic Records Society, 1980. List with ages, years resident, occupations, and notes on relationships. The diocese included the Deaneries of Kendal and Copeland. The Copeland list is also printed in: 'Papist returns, Deanery of Copeland, 1767', *C.F.H.S.N.* **36**, 1985, 15-17.

Unitarian

NICHOLSON, FRANCIS, & AXON, ERNEST. *The older nonconformity in Kendal: a history of the Unitarian chapel in the Market Place, with transcripts of the registers and notices of the nonconformist academies of Richard Frankland, M.A., and Caleb Rotheram, D.D.* Kendal: Titus Wilson, 1915. Includes register of baptisms and burials, 1687-1838, various lists of clergy, officers and members, and lists of pupils, together with many biographical notices.

13. ESTATE AND FAMILY PAPERS

A. *GENERAL*

The records of estate administration—deeds, leases, rentals, surveys, accounts, etc.—are a mine of information for the genealogist. Many of these records have been published in full or in part, although much more still lies untouched in the archives. The 'feet of fines', held in the Public Record Office, constitute one of the most important collections of deeds, and those for Cumberland have been edited in a number of works:

HUNTER, J., ed. *Fines sive pedes finium sive finales concordiae in curia domini regis, ab anno septimo regni regis Ricardi I ad annum decimum sextum regis Johannis A.D.1195-A.D.1214. Vol.2. in quo continentur comitatus Cumberl', Derb', Devon', et Dorset'.* George E. Eyre & Andrew Spottiswoode, 1844.

PARKER, F.H.M. 'A calendar of the feet of fines for Cumberland, from their commencement to the accession of Henry VII', *C.W.A.A.S., Tr.* N.S. **7**, 1907, 215-61.

HUDLESTON, C. ROY. 'Cumberland and Westmorland feet of fines in the reign of Henry VII', *C.W.A.A.S., Tr.* N.S. **66**, 1966, 159-64. 7 final concords.

STEEL, J.P. *Feet of fines, Cumberland, during the reign of Henry VIII.* Mitchell Hughes & Clarke, [191-?].

STEEL, J.P., ed. *Feet of fines, Cumberland, during the reigns of Edward VI, Mary, Philip & Mary, and Elizabeth.* Warren, Hall & Lovitt, [19—?].

A collection of Cumbrian deeds collected by a bookseller is calendared in:

WILSON, JAMES. 'Calendar of the original deeds at Tullie House, I: Latin', *C.W.A.A.S., Tr.* N.S. **14**, 1914, 63-82.

BOUCH, C.M. LOWTHER. 'Calendar of the original deeds at Tullie House, II', *C.W.A.A.S., Tr.* N.S. **38**, 1938, 245-66 & **39**, 1939, 136-51. Includes pedigree of Musgrave, 17th c.

Another booksellers collection is briefly listed in:

'The value of old parchment deeds in genealogical and topographical research', *Topographical quarterly* **4**(2), 1936, 165-6.

Many deeds from north of the Scottish border mention Cumbrian families. A calendar of such deeds is provided by:

REID, R.C., ed. *Wigtownshire charters.* Publication of the Scottish History Society 3rd series **51**, 1960. Medieval.

Miscellaneous estate records are printed in:

STEEL, J.P. 'Genealogical gleanings relating to Cumberland', *C.W.A.A.S., Tr.* N.S. **23**, 1923, 61-77. Relates to Sandwith, Lakenby, Penrith, Calder, etc., etc., also Cockermouth poll book, 1737.

The process of enclosing land from open field resulted in the creation of many documents. Enclosure awards usually include complete lists of landowners and tenants. Those for Cumberland are listed in:

TATE, W.E. 'A hand list of English enclosure acts and awards', *C.W.A.A.S., Tr.* N.S. **43**, 1943, 175-98.

B. *PRIVATE ESTATES*

Many families have preserved deeds and papers relating to their estates and their personal lives. Those which have been published are listed here.

By Family

Bagot

LYTE, H.C. MAXWELL. 'The manuscripts of Capt. Josceline F. Bagot', in HISTORICAL MANUSCRIPTS COMMISSION. *Tenth report,* appendix part IV. H.M.S.O., 1885, 318-47. Includes 12-13th c. Westmorland deeds and correspondence of Colonel James Graham, 17-18th c.

Birkbeck

HUDLESTON, C. ROY. 'Some Birkbeck documents', *C.W.A.A.S., Tr.* N.S. **63**, 1963, 184-98 & **64**, 1964, 214-8. Birkbeck family deeds relating to Hornby estate, 16-18th c.

Clifford

RAGG, FREDERICK W. 'The Feoffees of the Cliffords, from 1283 to 1482', *C.W.A.A.S., Tr.* N.S. **8**, 1908, 253-330. See also **22**, 1922, 329-45. Transcript of a 1482 Westmorland feodary, giving many names, 13-15th c., and including an extract from the lay subsidy roll, 1436, listing owners of lands worth more than 100/-.

WILLIAMSON, G.C. 'Lady Anne Clifford's account-book for 1665 and for 1667-8', *C.W.A.A.S., Tr.* N.S. **23**, 1923, 84-102. General discussion.

SCOTT, DANIEL. 'Recent discoveries in the muniment rooms of Appleby Castle and Skipton Castle', *C.W.A.A.S., Tr.* N.S. **18**, 1918, 189-210. Discussion of the Clifford family's muniments.

Crackenthorpe

HUDLESTON, C. ROY. 'Cumberland and Westmorland documents', *C.W.A.A.S., Tr.* N.S. **64**, 1964, 377-8. List of Crackenthorpe family deeds etc., medieval-18th c.

Dalston

HUDLESTON, C. ROY. 'Dalston family documents', *C.W.A.A.S., Tr.* N.S. **65**, 1965, 371-3. 17-18th c. commissions, deeds, etc., of Dalston family.

Elleray

ELLERAY, WILLIAM. 'Birkett Elleray of Winster', *C.F.H.S.N.* **54**, 1990, 13-18. List of names etc. in 17-19th c. estate papers of Elleray family.

Fallowfield

HUDLESTON, C. ROY. 'Some Fallowfield documents', *C.W.A.A.S., Tr.* N.S. **55**, 1955, 172-8. Deeds, 15-17th c., relating to the Fallowfield family; includes will of Thomas Fallowfield, 1630.

Fleming

COLLINGWOOD, W.G., ed. *The memoirs of Sir Daniel Fleming. C.W.A.A.S., T.S.* **11**, 1928. Includes many notes on estate administration, etc., 17th c.

Hird

'Edmond Hird, watch and clockmaker of Ambleside', *C.F.H.S.N.* **61**, 1991, 7-10. Accounts, 1889-90, naming many customers; also pedigree, 18-19th c.

Howard

ORNSBY, GEORGE, ed. *Selections from the household books of the Lord William Howard, of Naworth Castle, with an appendix containing some of his papers and other documents, illustrative of his life and times.* Surtees Society **68**, 1878. 1612-33.

HUDLESTON, C. ROY., ed. *Naworth estate and household accounts, 1648-1660.* Surtees Society **168**, 1958. Household book of the Howard family, primarily concerned with the Cumberland estates administered from Naworth.

Jackson

GRAINGER, FRANCIS. 'James Jackson's diary, 1650 to 1683', *C.W.A.A.S., Tr.* N.S. **21**, 1921, 96-129. Mainly accounts, 17th c., with many names from Holm Cultram and its area.

Kirkby

SCOTT, SIR S.H. 'A calendar of the papers and documents in the possession of Mr. James Burrow of Hill Top, Crosthwaite, near Kendal', *C.W.A.A.S., Tr.* N.S. **20**, 1920, 177-87. Calendar of 93 documents, 17-18th c., concerning the Crosthwaite and Furness districts, many relating to the Kirkby family.

Lowther

HAINSWORTH, D.R., ed. *Commercial papers of Sir Christopher Lowther, 1611-1644.* Surtees Society **189**, 1977. Includes pedigree of Lowther, 16-17th c.

PHILLIPS, C.B., ed. *Lowther family estate books, 1617-1675.* Surtees Society **191**, 1979. Includes rentals, 17th c. pedigree, etc.

HAINSWORTH, D.R., ed. *The correspondence of Sir John Lowther of Whitehaven, 1693-1698: a provincial community in wartime.* Records of social and economic history, N.S. **7**. Oxford University Press for the British Academy, 1983. Includes biographical notes on individuals referred to in the letters.

Meschens

See Tailbois

Pembroke

WHITESIDE, JOSEPH. 'Some accounts of Anne, Countess of Pembroke', *C.W.A.A.S., Tr.* N.S. **5**, 1905, 188-201. Household accounts, 1673, giving many names.

Tailbois

HODGSON, JOHN, ed. 'Ancient charters respecting monastical and lay property in Cumberland and other counties in the North of England ...', *Archaeologia Aeliana* **2**, 1832, 381-411. Includes medieval pedigree of Tailbois and Meschens families, to whom the charters relate.

By Place

Alston

NANSON, W. 'Notes on Alston manorial records', *C.W.A.A.S., Tr.* **8**, 1886, 29-39. General discussion of 16th c. records.

Aspatria

'Fines and admittances: Aspatria, 1634', *C.F.H.S.N.* **42**, 1987, 12-13. Lists tenants.

Barton

RAGG, FREDERICK W. 'Early Barton: its subsidiary manors and manors connected therewith', *C.W.A.A.S., Tr.* N.S. **24**, 1924, 295-350. 14 medieval deeds.

Beetham

HUTTON, WILLIAM. *The Beetham repository, 1770.* ed. John Rawlinson Ford. *C.W.A.A.S., T.S.* **7**, 1906. Includes many deeds, will extracts, inquisitions, pedigrees, subscription lists, etc.

Broad Oak
JONES, G.P. 'The Broad Oak deeds', *C.W.A.A.S., Tr.* N.S. **64**, 1964, 138-49. 17-18th c. deeds; includes will of Stephen Garnett, 1680.

Cliburn
RAGG, FREDERICK W. 'Cliburn Hervey and Cliburn Tailbois', *C.W.A.A.S., Tr.* N.S. **25**, 1925, 331-45 & **28**, 1928, 179-92. Includes calendar of 43 medieval documents relating to Cliburn, including an extensive rental of 1366 listing tenants; also much on the families of Hervey and Tailbois, and pedigrees of Cliburn and Fraunces.

Crosthwaite
WILSON, JAMES. 'Charters of Crosthwaite', *Northern notes and queries* **1**, 1906, 79-83, 106-14 & 145-52. Abstracts of 111 medieval deeds concerning Crosthwaite, from the chartulary of Fountains Abbey, Yorkshire.

Dalston
WILSON, JAMES. *The inclosure of the moors, commons and waste lands of Dalston, Cumberland.* Dalston: Beck, 1898. Includes award, giving names of proprietors, 1807.

Debateable Land
SANDERSON, ROUNDELL PALMER., ed. *Survey of the Debateable and Border lands adjoining the realm of Scotland and belonging to the Crown of England, taken A.D.1604.* Alnwick: [ ], 1891. Gives names of tenants, etc., in Cumberland and Northumberland.

Dunnerdale
'Dunnerdale rental for 1703', *C.F.H.S.N.* **6**, 1978, 18. Gives names of tenants.

Egremont
CAINE, CAESAR. 'The manor court of Egremont', *C.W.A.A.S., Tr.* N.S. **15**, 1915, 76-89. Includes extracts from 18th c. court rolls, giving some names.

Eskdale
See Kenniside

Farlam
'Tenants of Farlam manor, 1702', *C.F.H.S.N.* **35**, 1985, 14.

Gilsland
GRAHAM, T.H.B., ed. *The barony of Gilsland: Lord William Howard's survey, taken in 1603.* *C.W.A.A.S., E.S.* **16**, 1934.

Gosforth
THOMPSON, W.N. 'Gosforth in the chartulary of St.Bees', *C.W.A.A.S., Tr.* N.S. **2**, 1902, 307-21. Notes on medieval deeds.

Grasmere
'Manor of Grasmere court baron, 20 die September 1692', *C.F.H.S.N.* **30**, 1984, 23-5. Many names of tenants.

Grinsdale
COLLINGWOOD, W.G. 'A calendar of Grinsdale and Kirkandrews documents, 1635-1817', *C.W.A.A.S., Tr.* N.S. **22**, 1922, 252-80. Deeds.

Hutton John
COLLIGAN, J. HAY. 'The manor of Hutton John in 1668', *C.W.A.A.S., Tr.* N.S. **10**, 1910, 29-38. Includes list of tenants.

Kendal Barony
FARRER, WILLIAM. *Records relating to the Barony of Kendale.* ed. John F. Curwen. *C.W.A.A.S., R.S.* **4-6**, 1923-6. The barony covered the parishes of Kendal, Grasmere, Windermere, Heversham, Beetham, Burton, and Kirkby Lonsdale. These volumes include extracts from numerous documents at the Public Record Office—mainly deeds, inquisitions post mortem, tax records, etc.

Kenniside
M., S.M. 'Tenants for 1754', *C.F.H.S.N.* **11**, 1979, 16-17. At Kenniside, Wasdale and Eskdale.

Kirkandrews
See Grinsdale

Kirkby Lonsdale
CONDER, EDWARD. 'Some notes on the manors of Mansergh and Rigmaden, formerly in the parish of Kirkby Lonsdale', *C.W.A.A.S., Tr.* **14**, 1897, 450-59. With extracts from manorial records, including a list of tenants, 1750; also a pedigree of Godsalve, 17-19th c.

Kirklinton
'From a Kirklinton tailor's account book', *C.F.H.S.N.* **28**, 1983, 1-3 & **29**, 1983, 18-21. Lists customers, 1895-1915.

Mardale
See Threlkeld

Millom
WINCHESTER, ANGUS J.L. 'The castle household and demesne farm at Millom in 1513-14', *C.W.A.A.S., Tr.* N.S. **83**, 1983, 85-99. Accounts, giving many names.

Estate and Family Papers continued

Morland. Newby Stones
SMITH, BARBARA. 'Lonsdale papers at Carlisle R.O.', *C.F.H.S.N.* **23**, 1982, 16. Lists tenants of the manor of Newby Stones, Morland, 1702.

Rosgill
See Shap

Shap
RAGG, FREDERICK W. 'Shap and Rosgill and some of the early owners', *C.W.A.A.S., Tr.* N.S. **14**, 1914, 1-62. Includes many deeds, and medieval pedigree of de Rosgill and de Thornburgh.

Threlkeld
SIMPSON, GERTRUDE M. 'Townfields at Threlkeld, Mardale, Wet Sleddale and Langdale', *C.W.A.A.S., Tr.* N.S. **29**, 1929, 269-72. Includes maps of Threlkeld, 1848, and Mardale, 1842, giving names of occupiers (and owners of 1928 in the case of Threlkeld).

Torver
See Muchland

Wasdale
See Kenniside

Windermere
BROWNE, GEORGE. 'An award of 1535 relating to Adelaide Hill, Windermere; the boundaries of the manor of Windermere in 1614, and a rental of 1675', *C.W.A.A.S., Tr.* N.S. **14**, 1914, 298-302.

C. *ECCLESIASTICAL ESTATES AND CHARTULARIES, etc.*

In the medieval period, a great deal of property was owned by ecclesiastical institutions such as churches, monasteries, dioceses, etc. A number of cartularies, that is, collections of deeds, relating to Cumberland and Westmorland are in print:

Byland
BURTON, JANET. 'Charters of Byland Abbey relating to the Grange of Bleatarn, Westmorland', *C.W.A.A.S., Tr.* N.S. **79**, 1979, 29-50. 59 medieval deeds.

Furness
BROWNBILL, JOHN, ed. *The coucher book of Furness Abbey, volume II, part II.* Chetham Society, N.S. **76**, 1916. Furness was a Lancashire monastery, but owned much property in Cumberland; this volume includes many deeds relating to Meals, Kirksanton, Millom, Butterilket, Borrowdale and Cockermouth, Cumberland.

Holm Cultram
GRAINGER, FRANCIS, & COLLINGWOOD, W.G., eds. *The register and records of Holm Cultram.* *C.W.A.A.S., R.S.* **7**, 1929. Chartulary.

Lanercost
FERGUSON, CHARLES JOHN, WHITEHEAD, H., & BROWN, G. BALDWIN. *Lanercost Priory, with appendix of notes on the Dacres of Lanercost.* Carlisle: Thurnam, 1893.

WALCOTT, MACKENZIE E.C. 'Breviate of the cartulary of Lanercost', *Royal Society of Literature transactions* 2nd series **8**, 1866, 434-524.

Saint Bees
WILSON, JAMES, ed. *The register of the Priory of St.Bees.* Surtees Society **126**, 1915. Also issued as *C.W.A.A.S., R.S.* **3**.

Wetheral
PRESCOTT, J.E., ed. *The register of the Priory of Wetherhal.* C.W.A.A.S., R.S. **1**, 1897. Chartulary, with a rental of 1490, and various other medieval documents.

PRESCOTT, J.E. 'Notes on the manuscript register of Wetherhal, recently restored to the Dean and Chapter of Carlisle', *C.W.A.A.S., Tr.* **15**, 1899, 285-7. 14th c. cartulary.

D. *MANORIAL DESCENTS, etc.*

Many works which trace the descent of manors and other property have been published, and are listed here. A general volume which includes many notes on the descent of property is:

TAYLOR, MICHAEL WAISTELL. *The old manorial halls of Westmorland and Cumberland.* *C.W.A.A.S., E.S.* **8**, 1892.

A more restricted area is covered by:

GRAHAM, T.H.B. 'The Border manors', *C.W.A.A.S., Tr.* N.S. **11**, 1911, 38-54. Traces the medieval descent of Border manors, and includes folded pedigrees of Musgrave and other families.

Bewcastle
GRAHAM, T.H.B. 'The lords of Bewcastle', *C.W.A.A.S., Tr.* N.S. **29**, 1929, 57-68. Descent of the lordship.

Blakhale
GRAHAM, T.H.B. 'The manor of Blakhale', *C.W.A.A.S., Tr.* N.S. **18**, 1918, 125-30. Descent of the manor.

Estate and Family Papers *continued*

Bromfield. Rectory

TREVELYAN, W.C. 'Some account of the rectory of Bromfield, in the county of Cumberland', *Archaeologia Aeliana* 2, 1832, 171-6. Traces the 16-17th c. descent of Bromfield Rectory, which became private property after the Reformation.

Burgh by Sands

STOREY, R.L. 'The manor of Burgh-by-Sands', *C.W.A.A.S., Tr.* N.S. 53, 1953, 119-30. Medieval descent.

Caldbeck. Greenrig

PARKIN, JOHN S. 'Greenrig, Caldbeck', *C.W.A.A.S., Tr.* N.S. 21, 1921, 234-6. Deeds, 16-19th c., relating primarily to the Greenup family, showing descent of Greenrig.

Calees

MAWSON, D.J.W. 'Calees: a Cumbrian farm and its owners', *C.W.A.A.S., Tr.* N.S. 72, 1972, 142-55. Descent, 18-20th c.

Cargo

GRAHAM, T.H.B. 'The manor of Cargo', *C.W.A.A.S., Tr.* N.S. 24, 1924, 50-56. Medieval descent; includes pedigree of De Ros, 13-15th c.

Cockermouth

CURWEN, JOHN F. 'Cockermouth Castle', *C.W.A.A.S., Tr.* N.S. 11, 1911, 129-58. Includes pedigree showing medieval descent through De Fortibus, Multon, Morville, etc.

GRAHAM, T.H.B. 'The Honour of Cockermouth', *C.W.A.A.S., Tr.* N.S. 29, 1929, 69-80. Medieval descent of the Honour, including pedigree of Lucy, 11-14th c.

Corby

GRAHAM, T.H.B. 'The manor of Corby', *C.W.A.A.S., Tr.* N.S. 14, 1914, 238-55. See also N.S. 28, 1928, 416-7. Descent of the manor; includes pedigrees of Corkeby, 12-14th c., Salkeld, 14-16th c., and Howard, 16-18th c.

Deansbiggin

CHIPPINDALL, W.H. 'Deansbiggin near Kirkby Lonsdale', *C.W.A.A.S., Tr.* N.S. 29, 1929, 242-7. Descent of the property through Middleton, Booth and Borrett, etc., 16-20th c.

Drigg

FAIR, MARY C. 'Notes on the manor of Drigg', *C.W.A.A.S., Tr.* N.S. 49, 1949, 105-9. Genealogical notes; medieval.

Duddon

JOHNSON, SUSAN. 'Two Duddon farms: Thrang and Hazlehead', *C.W.A.A.S., Tr.* N.S. 61, 1961, 238-48. Descents of farms, 18-19th c.

Edenhall

RAGG, FREDERICK W. 'The earlier owners of Edenhall', *C.W.A.A.S., Tr.* N.S. 13, 1913, 199-227. Includes pedigree showing descent through De Turp, Stapelton, Hilton, etc.

Gosforth Hall

PARKER, C.A., & CURWEN, J.F. 'Gosforth Hall', *C.W.A.A.S., Tr.* N.S. 3, 1903, 227-39. Traces descent, and includes a pedigree of Copley, 17-18th c.

Great Orton

BOUCH, C.M. LOWTHER. 'The manor and advowson of Great Orton from 1369', *C.W.A.A.S., Tr.* N.S. 40, 1940, 46-55. Includes descent of the manor, and inquisition post mortem of Richard Coldaill, 1563.

Johnby Hall

BROWN, HELEN WRIGHT. 'Johnby Hall', *C.W.A.A.S., Tr.* N.S. 32, 1932, 85-103. Descent of the Hall, with many extracts from Greystoke parish register.

Kendal Barony

CURWEN, JOHN F. 'Kendal Castle', *C.W.A.A.S., Tr.* N.S. 8, 1908, 84-94. Includes folded pedigree showing the medieval descent of the Barony of Kendal.

Levens Hall

BAGOT, ANNETTE. *Levens Hall, Westmorland, owned by Robin Bagot*. Norwich: Jarrold & Sons, 1963. Includes list of owners and occupiers.

WESTON, G.F. 'Levens Hall, Westmoreland', *Archaeological journal* 26, 1869, 97-120. Descent through Levins, Bellingham and Grahme.

Mauld's Meaburn

RAGG, FREDERICK W. 'Mauld's Meaburn and le Fraunces and de Hastings', *C.W.A.A.S., Tr.* N.S. 11, 1911, 321-42. 13th c.

RAGG, FREDERICK W. 'Mauld's Meaburn and Newby: de Veteripont, le Francys and de Vernon', *C.W.A.A.S., Tr.* N.S. 12, 1912, 312-402. Medieval; includes 20 deeds, etc., and a pedigree of Morville.

Melmerby

GRAHAM, T.H.B. 'The manor of Melmerby',
C.W.A.A.S., Tr. N.S. **17**, 1917, 16-25. Medieval
descent of the manor through Wigton, Parvyng
and Threlkeld.

Old Salkeld

GRAHAM, T.H.B. 'Old Salkeld', *C.W.A.A.S., Tr.*
N.S. **21**, 1921, 63-73. Medieval descent of the
tenement; includes pedigree of Salkeld.

Penrith

WATSON, GEORGE. 'Gerard Lowther's House,
Penrith: its purchase by him, descent and social
life associated with its subsequent owners',
C.W.A.A.S., Tr. N.S. **1**, 1901, 94-103. 16-18th c.

Rockcliff

GRAHAM, T.H.B. 'Rockcliff', *C.W.A.A.S., Tr.* N.S.
24, 1924, 57-65. Medieval descent.

14. RECORDS OF NATIONAL, COUNTY AND LOCAL ADMINISTRATION

A. *NATIONAL AND COUNTY*

The records of central and local government
provide much information of use to genealogists.
Official lists of names have already been
discussed, but many other records are also
available. A number of historians have compiled
lists of members of parliament, sheriffs, and
wardens of the Marches. Their works include:

HUDLESTON, C. ROY. *A history of the Shrievalty of
Cumberland.* Carlisle: Cumberland
Newspapers, 1969. Includes list of sheriffs.

DUCKETT, SIR G. 'The sheriffs of Westmorland,
with the early sheriffs of Cumberland',
C.W.A.A.S., Tr. **4**, 1880, 285-317. Medieval
lists.

BEAN, WILLIAM WARDELL. *The Parliamentary
representation of the six northern counties of
England: Cumberland, Durham, Lancashire,
Northumberland, Westmoreland and Yorkshire,
and their cities and boroughs from 1603 to
1886, with lists of members and biographical
notices.* Hull: Charles Henry Barnwell, 1890.

WASHINGTON, GEORGE S.H.L. *Early Westmorland
M.P.'s, 1258-1327. C.W.A.A.S., T.S.* **15**, 1959.
Biographical notices of 67 M.P.'s.

FERGUSON, RICHARD S. *Cumberland and
Westmorland M.P.'s from the Restoration to the
Reform Bill of 1867 (1660-1867).* Bell & Daldy,
1871. A narrative account, rather than
biographies—but includes much biographical
material.

STOREY, R.L. 'The wardens of the Marches of
England towards Scotland, 1377-1489', *English
historical review* **72**(285), 1957, 593-615.
Includes a list.

Many editions of administrative documents have
been published; those likely to be of genealogical
interest are listed here in rough chronological
order:

*The pipe-rolls, or, sheriff's annual accounts of the
revenues of the crown for the counties of
Cumberland, Westmorland and Durham,
during the reigns of Henry I, Richard I, and
John.* Newcastle: T. & J. Hodgson for the
Society of Antiquaries of Newcastle upon Tyne,
1847.

PARKER, F.H.M., ed. *The pipe rolls of Cumberland
and Westmorland, 1222-1260. C.W.A.A.S., E.S.*
12, 1905.

National, County and Local Administration
continued

BRYDSON, ARTHUR. 'Notes on the Westmorland assize roll of A.D.1256', *C.W.A.A.S., Tr.* N.S. **13**, 1913, 62-78. Includes extracts.

FRASER, C.M. *Northern petitions illustrative of life in Berwick, Cumbria and Durham in the fourteenth century.* Surtees Society **194**, 1981.

DUCKETT, SIR G. 'Extracts from the Cottonian mss. relating to border service', *C.W.A.A.S., Tr.* **3**, 1878, 206-14. Names of gentry liable for border service, 1512-37.

BAIN, JOSEPH, ed. *Calendar of letters and papers relating to the affairs of the Border of England and Scotland preserved in Her Majesty's Public Record Office.* 2 vols. Edinburgh: H.M. General Register House, 1894. Official letters and papers, 1560-1603.

HISTORICAL MANUSCRIPTS COMMISSION. *The manuscripts of S.H. Le Fleming, esq., of Rydal Hall.* 12th report, appendix, part VII. C.5889-iv. H.M.S.O., 1890. Papers of Sir Daniel Fleming, 17th c., mainly concerned with local administration.

[RAINE, JAMES, JUN.], ed. *Depositions from the castle of York relating to offences committed in the northern counties in the seventeenth century.* Surtees Society **40**, 1861. Relating to Cumberland, Westmorland, Northumberland and Yorkshire, 1640-90.

FOX, P.H. 'The note book of William Thomson of Thornflatt, Justice of the Peace for Cumberland during the Commonwealth', *C.W.A.A.S., Tr.* N.S. **14**, 1914, 158-95. Includes marriages, warrants, recognizances, notes of conviction, etc., 1650s; also records of surrenders and admittances of customary tenants of the manor of Thornflatt, 1737-1900.

DUCKETT, SIR G. 'Letter from the Cumberland and Westmorland sequestration commissioners to the Lord Protector Cromwell enclosing lists of delinquents in the two counties, and sums at which their estates were assessed', *C.W.A.A.S., Tr.* **5**, 1881, 1-4. List of royalists, 1655.

HAYHURST, K. 'Westmorland Record Office: removal orders, 1697-1818', *C.F.H.S.N.* **22**, 1982, 15 & **23**, 1982, 15-16. Details of 43 orders.

JARVIS, RUPERT C. *The Jacobite risings of 1715 and 1745.* Record series **1**. [Carlisle]: Cumberland County Council, 1954. Records of the Lord Lieutenant and Quarter Sessions, giving many names of rebels, 'suspected persons', etc.

'Removals of Cumbrians', *C.F.H.S.N.* **43**, 1987, 8. From Lancashire to Cumberland and Westmorland, 18th c. From the index to Quarter session records at Preston.

'Jurymen, 1726', *C.F.H.S.N.* **47**, 1988, 7-8. List of those qualified to serve in the West Ward of Westmorland.

JARVIS, RUPERT C. 'Westmorland in the Forty-Five, three manuscripts', *C.W.A.A.S., Tr.* N.S. **45**, 1945, 179-86. Includes assessments for trophy money made at Underbarrow and Bradleyfield, 1745-6, with names.

COWLEY, D.I. 'Persons in Cumberland who have obtained game certificates for 1844', *C.F.H.S.N.* **9**, 1978, 18 & **11**, 1979, 19.

'Quarter Sessions, Kendal, 1852', *C.F.H.S.N.* **36**, 1985, 14-15. List of persons fined for drunkenness.

B. PAROCHIAL AND MUNICIPAL ADMINISTRATION

The records of parochial government—the accounts of overseers, churchwardens and other parish officers, rate lists, deeds, etc., contain much information of genealogical value, and frequently include the names of the humblest members of society, who otherwise went unrecorded. Many extracts from municipal, parochial, and family accounts, giving names, may be found in:

DOUGLAS, AUDREY, & GREENFIELD, P., eds. *Cumberland, Westmorland, Gloucestershire.* Records of early English drama. Toronto: University of Toronto Press, 1986.

Cumberland and Westmorland municipal and parochial records have been the subject of many works. Some of those likely to be of genealogical interest are listed here:

Addingham

SWIFT, F.B. 'Addingham churchwardens' accounts, vol.1 (1690-1848)', *C.W.A.A.S., Tr.* N.S. **52**, 1952, 114-25. General discussion.

Appleby

BOUCH, C.M.L. 'Local government in Appleby in the 17th and 18th centuries', *C.W.A.A.S., Tr.* N.S. **51**, 1951, 147-69. Extracts from the minute book and other records.

Barton

R[USSELL], M.M. 'Plea for a bridge', *C.F.H.S.N.* **51**, 1989, 17-19. Petition signed by residents of Barton, Martindale, Hilton, Askham, Lowther and Whaile, Westmorland, 1685.

Carlisle

FERGUSON, R.S. 'An account of the Dormont book belonging to the Corporation of Carlisle', *C.W.A.A.S., Tr.* **6**, 1883, 297-304. Discusses a volume which includes deeds, apprenticeship indentures, etc.

FERGUSON, R.S., & NANSON, W., eds. *Some municipal records of the city of Carlisle ... C.W.A.A.S., E.S.* **4**, 1887. Extracts from numerous sources.

SHEPPARD, J. BRIGSTOCKE. 'The historical mss. of the mayor and corporation of Carlisle', in *Ninth report of the Royal Commission on Historical Manuscripts.* C.3773. H.M.S.O., 1883, 197-203.

Clifton

BOUCH, C.M.L. 'The church and churchwardens' accounts of Clifton, Westmorland', *C.W.A.A.S., Tr.* N.S. **49**, 1949, 156-65. General discussion.

Cockermouth

GILLBANKS, W.F. 'Extracts from the vestry book of All Saints, Cockermouth', *C.W.A.A.S., Tr.* **9**, 1888, 101-16. Includes some names.

Crosthwaite

ELSAS, MADELAINE. 'Deeds of the parish of Crosthwaite', *C.W.A.A.S., Tr.* N.S. **45**, 1945, 39-48. Four deeds concerning parochial administration, 16-17th c.

Egremont

CAINE, CAESAR. 'The borough court of Egremont', *C.W.A.A.S., Tr.* N.S. **17**, 1917, 48-74. 17-18th c., gives many names.

Eskdale

FAIR, MARY C. 'Some notes on the Eskdale twenty four book', *C.W.A.A.S., Tr.* N.S. **22**, 1922, 72-8. Lists tenants, 1587 and 1659.

Great Salkeld

BOUCH, C.M.L. 'The churchwardens' accounts of the parish of Great Salkeld', *C.W.A.A.S., Tr.* N.S. **49**, 1949, 134-41. Discussion with brief abstracts, 16-17th c.

BOUCH, C.M.L. 'Poor law documents of the parish of Great Salkeld', *C.W.A.A.S., Tr.* N.S. **49**, 1949, 142-7. Brief discussion, 16-18th c.

Great Strickland

BOUCH, C.M. LOWTHER. 'The book of the overseers of the poor in the township of Great Strickland, 1778-1835', *C.W.A.A.S., Tr.* N.S. **50**, 1950, 164-70. Brief discussion, including extracts relating to the Penrith family, etc.

Holm Cultram

GRAINGER, FRANCIS. 'The sixteen men of Holm Cultram', *C.W.A.A.S., Tr.* N.S. **3**, 1903, 172-213. Includes list of the foremen of the sixteen, 1588-1883, with many other names.

Kendal

LYTE, H.C. MAXWELL. 'The manuscripts of the Corporation of Kendal', in HISTORICAL MANUSCRIPTS COMMISSION *Tenth report, appendix, part IV.* H.M.S.O., 1885, 299-318.

RUSHFORTH, GEORGE. 'Churchwardens' accounts, Kendal', *C.W.A.A.S., Tr.* **9**, 1888, 269-83. 17th c., includes some names.

FERGUSON, RICHARD S., ed. *A boke off recorde or register, containing all the acts and doings within the town of Kirkbiekendall, beginning 1575 ... C.W.A.A.S., E.S.* **7**, 1892. Contains many lists of freemen, officers, apprentices, etc., 16-17th c.

Keswick

COLLINGWOOD, W.G., ed. *Elizabethan Keswick: extracts from the original account books, 1564-1577, of the German miners, in the archives of Augsburg. C.W.A.A.S., T.S.* **8**, 1912. Includes chapters on the Hechstetter family, and an extensive list of debtors and creditors, 1574.

Kirkby Stephen

BREAY, J. 'Kirkby Stephen churchwardens' accounts, 1658 to 1670', *C.W.A.A.S., Tr.* N.S. **54**, 1954, 165-83. Includes extracts, 1658-70, giving many names.

'Parish assessments of township in parish of Kirkby Stephen, in Co. Westmorland', *Topographical quarterly* **1**(1), 1932, 68-74. 18th c.

Lamplugh

DICKINSON, R.F. 'The Friendly Society of the inhabitants of the parish of Lamplugh and its neighbourhood', *C.W.A.A.S., Tr.* N.S. **66**, 1966, 418-31. Includes list of original contributors, 1788.

Millom
ROSE, MARJORIE W. 'The red and white quilt',
C.F.H.S.N. **34**, 1985, 2-3. List of names from a
quilt made c.1887-90 at Millom.

St.Bees
ADDY, JOHN. 'Financial problems of St.Bees
churchwardens', *C.W.A.A.S., Tr.* N.S. **76**, 1976,
133-43. Includes extracts from accounts, 1651
and 1653.

Shap
WHITESIDE, J. 'Paines made at Shap', *C.W.A.A.S.,
Tr.* N.S. **3**, 1903, 150-62. Orders from the
manorial court, 16-18th c., giving many names.

Watermillock
HODGSON, W. 'A century of paines, or, local
government in the time of the Stuarts, as
illustrated by extracts from *A paine book for the
hamlet of Weathermelock*', *C.W.A.A.S., Tr.* **7**,
1884, 27-47. Gives many names, 17-18th c.
'A purvay rate thro' the hamlet of Watermelock,
1789', *C.F.H.S.N.* **28**, 1983, 11-12. Many
names.

Whitehaven
JACKSON, WILLIAM. 'Whitehaven: its streets, its
principal houses and their inhabitants',
C.W.A.A.S., Tr. **3**, 1878, 348-80. In effect, a
survey of the town, giving many names.

Windermere
THOMPSON, B.L. 'The Windermere four and
twenty', *C.W.A.A.S., Tr.* N.S. **54**, 1954, 151-64.
Originally a select vestry; includes names,
mainly 18th c., also includes list of records of
select vestries throughout Cumbria (including
Furness).

15. EDUCATIONAL RECORDS

Educational records can be made to yield a great
deal of genealogical information. The names of
teachers, pupils, governors, and others associated
with particular schools can all be found. The most
useful source is, of course, school registers, which
often provide details of parentage. The list of
works below is not a comprehensive listing of
school histories; rather, it identifies those works
which are most likely to be of value to the
genealogist. Most identify names.

A general survey of Westmorland schools in 1676
is provided by:
WALLIS, P.J. 'Westmorland schools about 1676:
Christopher Wase's survey', *C.W.A.A.S., Tr.*
N.S. **67**, 1967, 168-85. See also **74**, 1974, 352-4.
Includes lists of schoolmasters of various
schools.

Links between Cumbria and Queen's College,
Oxford, are discussed in:
PINHORN, MALCOLM. 'The Cumbrian connection',
Genealogist's magazine **18**, 1975-6, 347-9.

Appleby
BUDDEN, LIONEL. 'Some notes on the history of
Appleby Grammar School', *C.W.A.A.S., Tr.*
N.S. **39**, 1939, 227-61. Includes list of
headmasters, 1397-1942, and some local names.
LEACH, R.E. 'Benefactors to the library, Appleby
Grammar School', *C.W.A.A.S., Tr.* **13**, 1895,
20-36. Includes list, 1739-96.

Barton
'Notes on the school stock of the Barton Free
Grammar School, near Penrith, Cumbria',
C.F.H.S.N. **6**, 1978, 6-9 & **7**, 1978, 2-5. Many
17th c. names.

Bromfield
BOUCH, C.M. LOWTHER. 'A deed of 1740, about the
Bromfield grammar school', *C.W.A.A.S., Tr.*
N.S. **44**, 1944, 147-50. Signatories of deed
provide an almost complete list of landowners
in the parish.

Carlisle
PRESCOTT, CHANCELLOR. 'The Grammar School of
Carlisle', *C.W.A.A.S., Tr.* N.S. **16**, 1916, 1-28.
Includes list of masters, 1578-1875, etc.
ROUTLEDGE, G.B., ed. *Carlisle Grammar School
memorial register, 1264-1924*. Carlisle:
Thurnam, 1924. Includes brief notes on
parentage. Many corrections are noted in:
ROBINSON, F.J.G. 'Notes on Carlisle Grammar
School register', *C.W.A.A.S., Tr.* N.S. **69**, 1969,
152-78.

Keswick

BROATCH, J. *Keswick School: a short account of Keswick School, together with reprints of the ancient decrees affecting the foundation.* [Keswick]: [The School], 1926. Includes 17th c. documents giving some names of people associated with the school.

Kirkby Stephen

'Grammar school boys', *C.F.H.S.N.* **58**, 1991, 9-11. List of pupils at Kirkby Stephen Grammar School, 1823-52.

Matterdale

WHITESIDE, J. 'Matterdale church and school', *C.W.A.A.S., Tr.* N.S. **1**, 1901, 235-55. Includes list of schoolmasters, mainly 19th c.

Maughanby

SWIFT, F.B. 'Maughanby School', *C.W.A.A.S., Tr.* N.S. **54**, 1954, 236-47. Includes list of masters, 17-19th c., with some biographical notes.

Penrith

JACKSON, JOHN. *The history of the Queen Elizabeth Grammar School, Penrith.* Penrith: Reeds, for the Quarter Centenary Committee, 1963. Includes brief list of records.

REANEY, PERCY H., ed. *Records of Queen Elizabeth Grammar School, Penrith. C.W.A.A.S., T.S.* **10**, 1915. Includes a wide range of documents giving many names of teachers, pupils, tenants, tradesmen, benefactors, and others connected with the school, 16-18th c.

St.Bees

ALDOUS, J.W. *St.Bees School, Cumberland: The roll of honour and the record of old St.Beghians who served their King and country in the Great War, 1914-1919.* Edinburgh: T. & A. Constable, 1921.

The story of St.Bees, 1583-1939: a souvenir of the 350th anniversary of the opening of St.Bees School. Buck & Wootton, 1939. Includes much biographical information on pupils, and list of headmasters.

Whitehaven

ROBINSON, F.J.G., & WALLIS, P.J. 'Some early mathematical schools in Whitehaven', *C.W.A.A.S., Tr.* N.S. **75**, 1975, 262-74. Includes list of 18th c. schoolmasters.

Wigton

REED, DAVID W., ed. *1815-1953: Friends School, Wigton, Cumberland.* Carlisle: Wigton Old Scholars Association, 1954. Includes list of staff and other school registers.

Windermere

Windermere Grammar School: a history. Kendal: Westmorland Gazette, 1936. Includes information on feoffees and some local families, e.g. Philipson and Bolton.

FAMILY NAME INDEX

PLACE NAME INDEX

AUTHOR INDEX

Abercrombie, J. 34
Addy, J. 57
Aldous, J.W. 58
Allen, H.J. 33
Alsop, R.M. 15
Annis, R.G. 8
Appleby, A.B. 8
Armstrong, A.M. 44
Armstrong, B. 15
Arnison, J. 14, 30
Arnison, MAJ. 17
Ashcroft, L. 41
Atkinson, G. 12
Atkinson, H.W. 15
Axon, E. 48

Bagot, A. 53
Bain, J. 20, 28, 55
Ballasis, E. 21
Barker, F.W. 21
Barnes, E.S. 19
Barnes, F. 11
Barnes, M. 24
Barrow in Furness, Bishop of 46
Baterden, J.R. 32
Bean, W.W. 54
Beastall, T.W. 23
Beckett, J. 14
Beckett, J.V. 8, 9, 41
Bellasis, E. 23, 26, 38
Bewley, E.T. 16, 23
Birkbeck, R. 16
Birley, E. 21
Birley, R.N. 32
Bonsall, B. 9
Borradaile, A.F. 16
Borrow, J.R.E. 17
Bouch, C.M.L. 7, 16-18, 20, 22, 23, 26, 27, 46, 49, 53, 55-57
Bouch, J.L. 40
Boulton, C.H. 36
Boumphrey, R.S. 12, 13, 39, 40
Bower, R. 38
Boyes, Dr. 37
Breay, J. 47, 56
Brierly, H. 30-34
Broatch, J. 58
Brockett, W.H. 15
Brown, G.B. 39, 52

Brown, H.W. 53
Brown, J. 27
Brown, R.P. 16, 28, 40, 47
Brownbill, J. 52
Browne, G. 47, 52
Browne, W. 31
Brunskill, J. 17
Brydson, A. 47, 55
Budden, L. 57
Bulmer, T. 43
Burgess, J. 48
Burn, R. 7
Burton, J. 52

Caine, C. 32, 46, 51, 56
Cannon, R. 14
Carleton, L. 17
Carlisle and District Chamber of Trade 44
Carruthers, A.S. 17
Cherry, J. 11
Chippindall, W.H. 16, 25, 53
Clark, G.T. 24
Clark, P. 8
Clay, C. 41
Clay, J.W. 35
Cockerill, T. 15, 36
Cockerill, T.J. 16
Collier, S. 9
Colligan, J.H. 48, 51
Collingwood, W.G. 7, 11, 36, 50-52, 56
Collingwood, W.T. 19
Conder, E. 33, 41, 51
Cookson, E. 29
Cooper, G.M. 18
Coulthard, J. 18
Cowley, D.I. 15, 40, 55
Cowper, H.S. 21, 22, 37, 40
Cox, J.C. 45
Cresswell, L. 23
Cropper, J. 20
Crosfield, J.F. 18
Crossfield, H.E. 20
Crosthwaite, J.F. 14, 17, 31
Cumbria Family History Society 12, 29, 34, 36, 42
Curwen, A.D. 18
Curwen, J.F. 7, 10, 12, 16-19, 27,

44, 47, 51, 53
Curwen, P. 32
Curwen, S.P. 35

Darlow, G.S. 25
Davey, C.R. 17, 46
Davidson, E. 26
Davies-Shiel, M. 7
Dearden, J. 28
Denton, J. 8
Denyer, S. 8
Dickens, A.G. 18
Dickins, B. 44
Dickinson, J.C. 37
Dickinson, R. 32, 56
Dickinson, W. 45
Dixon, C.J. 40
Dixon, P. 23
Donal, G. 48
Douglas, A. 55
Duckett, G. 7, 10, 19, 24, 54, 55
Dudbridge, J. 36
Duke, J.E. 28
Duxbury, A. 9
Dyhouse, C.A. 9

Eeles, F.C. 46
Elleray, W. 50
Elsas, M. 56
Eshelby, H.D. 36
Evans, J. 37
Evans, M. 25
Ewbank, J.M. 7

Fahy, T.G. 16, 18, 21, 24, 25
Fair, M.C. 29, 53, 56
Faraday, M.A. 41
Farrer, W. 51
Fell, A.L. 20
Ferguson, C.J. 52
Ferguson, M.J. 39
Ferguson, R.S. 7, 8, 12, 31, 33, 35, 37, 39, 40, 45, 46, 48, 54, 56
Fetherston, J. 12
Fetherstonhaugh, Mrs. 20
Field, F.J. 12, 39
Finlay, M. 14
Fleming, D. 7
Fleming, J. 20